INTRODUCTION

The state of Israel was founded in 1948 following a war which the Israelis call the War of Independence, and the Palestinians call the *Nakba*—the catastrophe. A haunted, persecuted people sought to find a shelter and a state for itself, and did so at a horrible price to another people. During the war of 1948, more than half of the Palestinian population at the time—1,380,000 people—were driven off their homeland by the Israeli army. Though Israel officially claimed that a majority of the refugees fled and were not expelled, it still refused to allow them to return, as a UN resolution demanded shortly after the 1948 war. Thus, the Israeli land was obtained through ethnic cleansing of the indigenous Palestinian inhabitants.

This is not a process unfamiliar in history. Israel's actions remain incomparable to the massive ethnic cleansing of Native Americans by the settlers and government of the United States. Had Israel stopped there, in 1948, I could probably live with it. As an Israeli, I grew up believing that this primal sin our state was founded on may be forgiven one day, because the founders' generation was driven by the faith that this was the only way to save the Jewish people from the danger of another holocaust.

But it didn't stop there. In 1967, following a comprehensive war with three neighboring Arab countries, Israel conquered and occupied the West Bank (from Jordan), the Gaza Strip and the Sinai Peninsula (from Egypt), and the Golan Heights (from Syria). The Sinai Peninsula was eventually returned to Egypt, in a framework of a peace agreement between the two countries. (Israeli withdrawal was completed in 1982.) The rest of the territories acquired in 1967 are still occupied by Israel. During the 1967 war, a new wave of Palestinian refugees escaped from the West Bank and the Gaza Strip. (The number, according to Israeli sources, was 250,000 people.). About three million Palestinians still live in these two areas today, under Israeli occupation, surrounded by Israeli settlements built on their land.

Renowned Israeli philosopher and scientist Yeshayahu Leibovitz warned of what the occupation would lead to right from the start. In 1968 he wrote: "A state governing a hostile population of 1.5 to 2 million foreigners [the number of the Palestinians in the occupied territories at the time] is bound to become a Shin Bet [Security Service] state, with all that this implies for the spirit of education, freedom of speech and thought and democracy. Israel will be infected with corruption, characteristic of any colonial regime. The administration will have to deal with the suppression of an Arab protest

Tanya Reinhart

movement on the one hand, and with the acquisition of Arab quislings on the other...The army, which has been so far a people's army, will degenerate as well by becoming an occupation army, and its officers, turned into military governors, will not differ from military governors elsewhere in the world."[1]

In the power-drunk atmosphere which prevailed in Israel at the time, not many people paid attention to Leibowitz's warnings. U.S.-Israeli relations improved after Israel's military victory in 1967, which proved that Israel was a valuable strategic asset for U.S. interests in the region. Backed by the U.S., Israel felt omnipotent.[2] In 1982, then-defense minister Ariel Sharon led Israel into a new adventure in Lebanon with the ambitious goals of creating a "new order" in the Middle East, destroying the Palestinian Liberation Organization—which had developed in the Palestinian refugee camps in Lebanon, and gaining permanent control over Southern Lebanon, which borders with Israel. The attack left over 11,000 Lebanese and Palestinians dead.[3] Even though Israeli society perceived the war with Lebanon as a failure, the Israeli military stayed in the conquered land of Southern Lebanon until May 2000. Israel's occupation of the Palestinian land acquired in 1967 continued undisturbed.

The first Palestinian uprising (1987–1993) brought a change. Israeli society discovered that its military occupation of Palestinian land had a heavy price. Many realized that Leibovitz's warning was becoming reality, and many could no longer accept the occupation on moral grounds. On the Palestinian side, the struggle for independence was also based—for the first time—on explicit recognition of Israel's right to exist (in its pre-1967 borders). As we shall see, the Intifada Meeting of the Palestine National Council in 1988 called for the partition of the historical Palestine to two independent states. The struggle against the occupation became a joint Israeli-Palestinian struggle, with many Israeli opposition groups demonstrating in the territories, or inviting Palestinian leaders to speak at teach-ins in Israeli universities. In one of the many events of that joint struggle, twenty-seven members of the Israeli "21st Year" movement (including myself) were jailed for five days following a demonstration in the West Bank.

By 1993, it seemed that the occupation was reaching its end. Many believed that the Oslo Accords, signed in Washington that year, would lead to Israel's withdrawal from the occupied territories and the formation of a Palestinian state. But this is not how things turned out. As we shall see, the political leadership of the Israeli peace camp has turned the Oslo spirit of reconciliation into a new and more sophisticated form of maintaining the occupation.

Sharon, now Israel's prime minister, describes its present war against the Palestinians as "the second half of 1948." Israeli military echelons had already used the same description in October 2000, at the outset of the second Intifada—the present Palestinian uprising. By now, there can be little doubt that what they mean by that analogy is that the work of ethnic cleansing was only half completed in 1948, leaving too much land to Palestinians. Although the majority of Israelis are tired

Tanya Reinhart

of wars and of the occupation, Israel's political and military leadership is still driven by the greed for land, water resources, and power. From that perspective, the war of 1948 was just the first step in a more ambitious and more far-reaching strategy.

This book focuses on the post-Oslo era, and follows Israel's policies in the three years since Ehud Barak became prime minister, until the summer of 2002—the darkest period in the history of Israel so far. As we shall see, the shift in Israeli policy at this period was neither a spontaneous reaction to terror nor an act of self-defense, but calculated plans, systematically executed. The book is an updated and expanded version of my *Détruire la Palestine, ou comment terminer la guerre de 1948*, which appeared in French in April 2002 (France: La Fabrique, 2002). *Détruire la Palestine* examined (inter alia) the development of Israeli plans to destroy the Palestinian Authority. In the period between April 2002 and July 2002, these plans were fully executed.

Note: The book is based mainly on sources from the Israeli media, though other sources are cited as well. Of the Israeli Hebrew papers, only *Ha'aretz* has an Internet English version, which I used for most quotes from *Ha'aretz*. For the other Israeli papers, the quotes are my translation of the original Hebrew. In a few cases, where I could not check the English version of a piece that appeared in *Ha'aretz* in Hebrew, the quote is marked as "author's translation." Since approximately April 2002, *Ha'aretz*'s English version appears to be more heavily censored than its Hebrew version, and certain quoted items appeared only in the Hebrew version. These are marked as "Hebrew edition only."

MIDDLE EAST

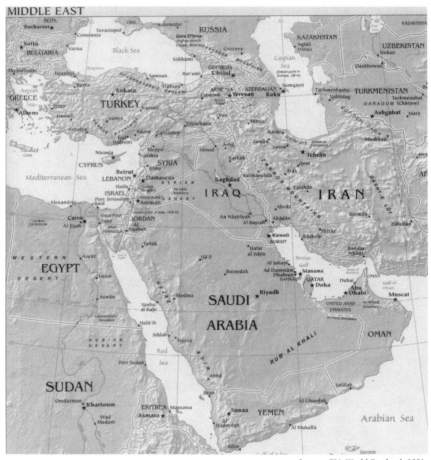

Source: CIA World Factbook 2001

CHAPTER I

THE OSLO YEARS: FALSE EXPECTATIONS

Israel—parroted by mainstream Western media—describes its handling of the Palestinian uprising as a war of defense: The Palestinians are terrorists—they are a violent, noncompromising, fanatical people who reject Israel's generous peace offers. Whatever you give them, Israel argues, they always want more; they are extremists who are willing to kill their children just to gain a few centimeters of what they view as their own land, and their true goal is to "push the Israelis into the sea." As former prime minister Ehud Barak put it, "I have not yet managed to understand from Arafat that he is willing to acknowledge the existence of the state of Israel."[4]

But just stop and recall. These are the same Palestinians who in the early 1990's offered their hands in peace to Israel. In September 1993, the Oslo Accords were signed at a ceremony at the White House, which many took to be the start of a new era of reconciliation. For most Palestinians,

September 1993 was a month of euphoria and optimism. Members of the PLO Hawks—the local military units of the PLO—returned their arms, and were interviewed on Israeli TV speaking of the new era of peace and living side by side as good neighbors. There was much talk about how similar and close these two peoples are. There was a real feeling that a new chapter had opened and that the past would be forgiven.

The ceremony at the White House was the climax of a process that had started much earlier. For many years, there were two lines of thought in Palestinian society. One called for the Palestinians to resist anything less than regaining the whole of Palestine, and even to "let the Jews be thrown into the sea"; the other called for a solution based on recognizing the rights of both nations, and emphasized the need to find a model for coexistence between the two peoples. From the Palestinian perspective, accepting the idea of two states has been an enormous concession, one that involves giving up almost 80 percent of the historical Palestinian homeland. (The West Bank and Gaza Strip only make up 22 percent of the historical Palestine, but that 22 percent is the only territory now under discussion as the future Palestinian state.)

Even during the worst periods of oppression in the occupied territories, when their position was far from popular, the secular leadership and the local PLO institutions, as well as independent intellectuals, human rights activists, and workers unions, were calling for cooperation with the Israeli peace forces opposing the occupation.

Since at least 1988, a majority of Palestinian society subscribed to this line. In November 1988, at the peak of the first Palestinian Intifada (uprising), the nineteenth session of the Palestine National Council (PNC)—the top forum of all Palestinian organizations—was held in Algiers under the title "Intifada Meeting." In an overwhelming majority vote of 253 to 46, it passed unequivocal resolutions accepting the partition of the historical Palestine, in which a Palestinian and an Israeli state would coexist along the lines of the pre-1967 borders, as determined by UN resolutions 181, 242, and 338. The PNC's resolutions called for a peaceful settlement of the conflict, and denounced terrorism in all its forms. An enthusiastic Edward Said, who was present at the historic meeting said, "Most of us there had grown up with the reality (lived and remembered) of Palestine as an Arab country, refusing to concede anything more than the exigency of a Jewish state, won at our expense in the loss of our land, our society, and literally uncountable thousands of lives. A million and a half of our compatriots were under brutal military occupation.... For the first time, also, the declarations were implicitly recognizing a state that offered us nothing whatever."[5]

The six years of the first Palestinian uprising (1987–1993) convinced the majority of Israelis that maintaining the occupation is unfeasible. Combined with the victory of the reconciliation line in Palestinian society, many people felt for the first time that a two-state solution might be realistic. September 1993 was also a euphoric month for many Israelis. The dominant public perception was that the occupation was over and a Palestinian state was imminent. Israel's right wing and settlers reacted with true panic, and the rest with a new, almost unfamiliar, sense of optimism. During those first couple of months after Oslo, most Israelis believed that the settlements were going to be dismantled and prices of apartments in central Israel shot up in expectation for the wave of relocating settlers. Nevertheless, in the polls two-thirds of the Israelis supported Oslo.

But that's not how things turned out. By 2000—seven years after the Oslo Accords were signed—the situation was worse than it had ever been. It is particularly revealing to see what happened in the Gaza Strip, as Gaza was the subject of substantial consensus in Israeli society before Oslo. With one million people living in one of the most densely populated and poorest areas of the world, with little water or natural resources, "What do we need Gaza for?" was a common question in Israel for years.

Nevertheless, during the Oslo negotiations, Israel insisted that it would not dismantle any settlements in Gaza, at least during the five-year "interim period." The Palestinian negotiators agreed to this condition when they signed the Oslo Accords at the White House ceremony. Yitzhak Rabin's insistence was not driven by popular pressure. Many of the settlers in the more isolated settlements wanted, in fact, to leave at the time, and demanded compensation for alternative housing. But Rabin refused.

What followed was worse. In the Taba negotiations just a month after the White House ceremony, Israel presented its

actual maps for Gaza, which left much more than the settlements under full Israeli control. Israel insisted that the settlements would be grouped in three blocs that would also include
the lands between the individual settlements. Combined with
a rich network of bypass roads, these blocs amount to over
one-third of the land in the Gaza Strip. The Palestinian negotiators responded with what appeared to be shock and anger.
Nabil Sha'at described the proposal as a "Swiss cheese" plan
for the cantonization of Gaza. The Palestinian delegation left
in protest, and the crisis appeared serious.[6]

But two weeks later, in talks in Cairo on November 18,
1993, the Palestinian negotiators fully accepted all the
Israeli demands. That first sweeping Palestinian surrender
marked the beginning of a long series of negotiations in
which Israel dictated and Arafat protested, cried, and signed.

The process through which a leader of a national liberation movement is coerced into collaboration is a long and
complex one. On the eve of Oslo, Yasser Arafat's grip on the
territories was deteriorating—as well as his control over the
refugee camps in Lebanon and in Jordan. In the occupied territories, there were daily complaints and protests regarding
the corruption of his aides in Tunis, his undemocratic rule,
and his sole control over the organization's finances. The
local Palestinian delegation headed by Haidar Abd-el Shafi
was gaining much more respect in the territories than
Arafat's anachronistic administration. A major victory was
the only thing that could then save him, and the Oslo agreements initially seemed to be just such a victory. While the

local Palestinian delegation insisted in its negotiations with Israel that it would not accept any agreement that didn't include immediate dismantlement of the Israeli settlements in the Gaza Strip, Arafat signed such an agreement behind its backs.

Arafat's shaky position was also obvious to the Israeli side. The prevailing interpretation of the early Oslo negotiations is that Rabin —the architect of the Oslo process— intended the process to lead eventually to full Israeli withdrawal from the occupied territories, which he may have viewed as a necessary response to changing public opinion in Israel. By this interpretation, it is hard to explain why he insisted, from the start, on keeping the Gaza settlements and expanding the areas they control. But even if he originally had such intentions, Rabin could not resist the opportunity provided by Arafat's weakness of turning this unique historical moment into a heightened form of Israeli domination and control.

The situation in Gaza today is that six thousand Israeli settlers occupy about one-third of the area (including the military bases and bypass roads), and one million Palestinians are squeezed into the other two thirds. Surrounded by electronic fences and military posts, tightly sealed from the outside world, Palestinian Gaza has turned into a massive prison ghetto. The standards of living in Gaza, which were already among the lowest in the world, have deteriorated sharply since Oslo. Until Oslo, it was possible for Palestinian Gaza residents to obtain exit permits.

Since Oslo, they are not even allowed to visit their relatives in the West Bank, and only a lucky few carry exit permits for work in Israel.

Possibly Israel intended to allow the Palestinians, in some future time, to call their prison "the Palestinian state," but the overall dynamic of Israeli domination would remain the same. If the prisoners try to rebel, as is happening now, the internal roads are blocked and the area is divided into smaller prison units, each surrounded by Israeli tanks. The Palestinian prisoners can be bombarded from the air, with nowhere to escape to; their food supply, electricity, and fuel are all controlled by Israel and cut off at the will of the prison guards. Israel has given the Palestinians in Gaza one choice: Accept prison life, or perish.

Israel's efforts have since focused on extending the Gaza arrangement to the West Bank. By September 2000, the Palestinians' areas were already split into four isolated enclaves—surrounded by Israeli settlements, military posts, and bypass roads. Many Israeli settlements already form massive blocs ready for annexation, though there are also many isolated settlements in the midst of the Palestinian population. (For more on the Oslo realities, see the Appendix.[7])

Seven years after Oslo, nothing was left of the hopes and expectations that the agreements had raised for so many people. Israel had a historical opportunity to reach a just peace with the Palestinian people and to integrate into the Middle East. Instead, it began a new chapter of oppression and control. It soon became obvious that the situation in the territories could eventually explode when the Palestinians realized that after years of humiliating negotiations, all they were going to get were vague promises that would never be kept.

But during all these years Israel's official line has been that the situation is temporary. According to this line, the Oslo agreement and those that followed it were just interim agreements—necessary steps in the long process required for working out the details of a final agreement. At least the Labor governments, which depend on the votes of those who have long been fed up with the occupation, kept pledging that at the end of the interim period, a new era would start. Their promise was compelling: Israel would eventually withdraw, end the occupation, and a Palestinian state would be formed in the West Bank and Gaza.

In July 2000, a Labor prime minister—Ehud Barak—led the Israelis and the world to believe that Israel was willing to start, finally, this new era of peace.

CHAPTER II

THE CAMP DAVID NEGOTIATIONS: MYTHS AND FACTS

The Camp David Summit of July 2000 has been perceived as a turning point in Israeli-Palestinian relations. The Israeli perspective, shared by both doves and hawks, was that Barak "broke every imaginable taboo" and offered concessions that no Israeli prime minister offered before, or could possibly offer again in the future. According to this version of the story, Barak offered to return 90 percent of the occupied West Bank and all of the Gaza Strip to the Palestinians. All he wanted in return was to annex 10 percent of the land with the big settlement blocs, where 150,000 Israelis already had their home. Regarding the most sensitive issue of Jerusalem, to which the Israelis feel particularly attached, he took an enormous risk, agreeing to divide the city and recognize part of it as the capital of the future Palestinian state. However, according to this version of the story, the Palestinian negotiators rejected these generous proposals, and failed even to come up with constructive counterproposals. Thus, they not only missed another historical opportunity, but also betrayed their rooted unwillingness to accept the existence of the Jewish state, or live in peace with it. Hence, according to this version of things, Israel's new war of defense against the Palestinians was inevitable.

To date, that version of history is the one that has been adopted by the United States and reinforced by Western media. The power of constant repetition has given it the status of objective truth in many people's minds. The first cracks in the story began to appear a year later when U.S. official Robert Malley's revelations were published. Malley was special assistant for Arab-Israeli affairs to President Bill Clinton from 1998 to 2001 and participated in the Camp David negotiations. He took extensive notes at the time, and after a year of observing the silence of the West regarding Israel's brutality toward the Palestinians, he went public in a series of articles published in the *New York Times*. Malley wrote:

> Many have come to believe that the Palestinians' rejection of the Camp David ideas exposed an underlying rejection of Israel's right to exist. But consider the facts: The Palestinians were arguing for the creation of a Palestinian state based on the June 4, 1967, borders, living alongside Israel. They accepted the notion of Israeli annexation of West Bank territory to accommodate settlement blocs. They accepted the principle of Israeli sovereignty over the Jewish neighborhoods of East Jerusalem—

neighborhoods that were not part of Israel before the Six Day War in 1967. And, while they insisted on recognition of the refugees' right of return, they agreed that it should be implemented in a manner that protected Israel's demographic and security interests by limiting the number of returnees. No other Arab party that has negotiated with Israel— not Anwar el-Sadat's Egypt, not King Hussein's Jordan, let alone Hafez al-Assad's Syria—ever came close to even considering such compromises.[8]

Apart from the facts, the biggest distortion in the dominant perspective of Camp David has been the symmetry it imposes on the two sides—that they were both facing equal sacrifices that the rejectionist Palestinians were not willing to undertake. The Western world has great sympathy for the difficulties of Israel. In the eyes of Israel giving up even an inch of the occupied territories is an enormous sacrifice. It means renouncing dreams about the historical promised land where the ancestors of the Israeli people lived two thousand years ago. It is also a huge political sacrifice. Anybody willing to give up anything is risking right-wing agitation, and the Palestinians should understand this fragile dynamic ruling all Israeli governments.

What has gained far less attention and sympathy is the sacrifices of the Palestinian people. Their historical ties to the land are much more current than ancient biblical times. Up until 1948, the Palestinian people lived in the whole land of

Palestine/Israel. Many who remember their childhood homes there are still alive, and many others grew up with dreams and memories passed on by their parents. Still, they agreed to give up 78 percent of the homeland of their parents and elders. As I mentioned, the division of the country along the lines of the pre-1967 border would leave the Palestinians with 22 percent of what they view as their original land. They accepted that division in 1988, and reconfirmed it in Oslo. Since Oslo, mainstream Palestinian society has given up on armed struggle and even on political struggle to regain that land. For seven years the Palestinians kept waiting for Israel to carry out its pledge to return their 22 percent of the land. And during the wait, all the Palestinians would hear echoing from Israel and the West was that their sacrifice was still not enough.

Now let's look at the facts. Did Barak really offer—at Camp David or in later negotiations—what is attributed to him by the dominant Western view? To begin with, official claims about Barak's offers come with no documentation to substantiate them. As Akiva Eldar, a senior analyst at *Ha'aretz*, pointed out, "Hardly anyone has any idea what those understandings are. No one has seen the paper summarizing these understandings, because no such paper exists. Veteran diplomats cannot recall political talks whose content was not put down on paper."[9]

This is also confirmed by Malley's documentation:

> If there is one issue that Israelis agree on, it is that Barak broke every conceivable taboo and went as

far as any Israeli prime minister had gone or could go...Even so, it is hard to state with confidence how far Barak was actually prepared to go. His strategy was predicated on the belief that Israel ought not to reveal its final positions—not even to the United States—unless and until the endgame was in sight. Had any member of the U.S. peace team been asked to describe Barak's true positions before or even during Camp David—indeed, were any asked that question today—they would be hard-pressed to answer.... The final and largely unnoticed consequence of Barak's approach is that, strictly speaking, there never was an Israeli offer.... The Israelis always stopped one, if not several, steps short of a proposal. The ideas put forward at Camp David were never stated in writing, but orally conveyed. They generally were presented as U.S. concepts, not Israeli ones; indeed, despite having demanded the opportunity to negotiate face to face with Arafat, Barak refused to hold any substantive meeting with him at Camp David out of fear that the Palestinian leader would seek to put Israeli concessions on the record. Nor were the proposals detailed. If written down, the American ideas at Camp David would have covered no more than a few pages. Barak and the Americans insisted that Arafat accept them as general "bases for negotiations" before launching into more rigorous negotiations.[10]

Nevertheless, despite this smoke screen, much information that was omitted from the official history was leaked to the Israeli press. These leaks enable us to examine what Barak was actually willing to offer.

POINT OF DEPARTURE: THE BEILIN-ABU MAZEN PLAN

Barak's proposal at Camp David was based on a document known as the Beilin–Abu Mazen understandings.[11] This document was completed, after extensive secret negotiations, in the last week of October 1995, just days before a Jewish law student assassinated Prime Minister Yitzhak Rabin.[12] In Israeli discourse, the plan was described as a far-reaching concession, one that no Israeli prime minister was willing to accept, until Barak.

In fact, the Beilin–Abu Mazen Plan is a shameful document that leaves all the settlements untouched. On the eve of the Camp David summit—June 21, 2000—then Justice Minister Yossi Beilin presented the document to the cabinet meeting of the Israeli government. Its content, as summarized in *Ha'aretz*, was that Israel would withdraw from 90 to 95 percent of the West Bank: "About 130 settlements will remain under Israeli sovereignty, 50 will stay within the Palestinian state. In the Jordan Valley, which will be under Palestinian sovereignty, Israeli military forces will be posted. The Palestinian state will recognize Western Jerusalem

Tanya Reinhart

as the capital of Israel, while Israel will recognize that the [portion of the] area defined as 'Al-Quds' prior to the six days war which exceeds the area annexed to Israel in 1967 will be the capital of the Palestinian state...Temple Mount [Al-Aqsa complex] will be given to Palestinian Sovereignty..."[13]

Read briefly, the text may seem to include some Israeli concessions. What gives this impression is the statement that Israel will recognize Palestinian sovereignty over 90 to 95 percent of the West Bank. But a closer reading reveals a different picture. The question is what precisely Israel means by "sovereignty." Inside the Palestinian "sovereign area," fifty Israeli settlements will remain intact and Israeli forces will remain in the Jordan Valley. As we shall see directly, the complex language describing "Al-Quds" means that the Palestinian capital will be the remote village of Abu-Dis. A better picture of the plan can be drawn from how Beilin himself described it in an interview in March 1996:

> As an outcome of my negotiations, I can say with certainty that we can reach a permanent agreement not under the overt conditions presented by the Palestinians, but under a significant compromise [on their side]...I discovered on their side a substantial gap between their slogans and their actual understanding of reality—a much bigger gap than on our side. They are willing to accept an agreement which gives up much land, without the dis-

mantling of settlements, with no return to the '67 border, and with an arrangement in Jerusalem which is less than municipality level.[14]

A charitable interpretation of these understandings would be that its authors entertained the hope that, assuming the establishment of a real, independent Palestinian state in the future, it would be possible for the residents of fifty Jewish settlements to live in peace, as citizens of the new state, accepting its laws, and restricting themselves to the land they already sit on, just as Palestinians live within the green line as citizens of Israel. If so, it would take a blatant ignorance of the history of Israel and its recent politics to believe that Israel will give up the "defense needs" of these settlers, their land reserves, and the bypass roads connecting them to Israel. In fact, leaving these settlements intact would entail that 40 to 50 percent of the newly created state would consist of areas that Palestinians would have no access to.

The Israeli press described the cabinet meeting at which the Beilin-Abu Mazen understandings were presented as a historic event: "This was a dramatic moment in the history of the Israeli-Palestinian negotiations...For the first time, the top governmental forum has received a full report of the details of the understandings between the person who is considered Arafat's top confidant, and the person who was considered at the time Peres' top confidant. Though parts of the agreement were leaked before, it was the first time the cabinet members were given a chance learn its full details."[15]

As with anything surrounding the Camp David negotiations, the overall Israeli perception was that in accepting the line of the Beilin–Abu Mazen understandings, Israel was entering an era of unprecedented concessions. It is therefore interesting to observe the reaction of Nathan Sharansky, one of the most outspoken right-wing members of the government, who was notably against any concessions. Apparently surprised by how much the Palestinians were willing to give up, "Sharansky asked Beilin if he was sure that Abu Mazen shared these understandings, to which [the] Justice Minister answered: 'take your car, go half an hour to Ramallah and find out with him.'"[16]

This of course did not stop Sharansky from resigning later in protest of Israel's "concessions."

As we shall see, Barak's proposal at Camp David was just a worsened version of the Beilin–Abu Mazen plan. As far as it is known, this plan had already been approved by Arafat at the time it was conceived—though it is not clear to what degree Palestinian society was aware of its details. As with all other rounds of negotiations since Oslo, such details were carefully concealed from the Palestinian people. Information readily available in the Israeli press did not—and does not—make it to the Palestinian media, which is heavily censored by the Palestinian Authority.

That Arafat approved this shameful plan is not entirely surprising. His road of defeat and collaboration had started long before, on the eve of Oslo. Still, the implementation of the plan leaves much to the goodwill of Israel, and it is possible that Arafat hoped he would get a more favorable implementation of the plan than that which Barak tried to force on him at Camp David.

WHAT BARAK OFFERED AT CAMP DAVID

The crucial turning point at Camp David was that Barak demanded that the sides sign a "final agreement," accompanied by a Palestinian declaration of an "end of conflict." Had the Palestinians signed such a declaration, they would have lost all legal standing for future claims based on UN resolutions. Of course, Barak's demand was clothed in language that was hard to disagree with, as when he said, "If the Palestinians want to establish a state, they must first declare that the century-old Jewish-Arab conflict has come to an end." It is only the finale that clarifies that this is, in fact, a threat: "The alternative," Barak added, "is a bloody confrontation that would bring no gain."[17]

Up to the present, the abiding legal basis for negotiations has been UN resolutions—most notably Resolution 242, passed on November 22, 1967, which requires the "withdrawal of Israeli armed forces from territories occupied in the recent conflict," but also Resolution 194 of December 11, 1948, regarding the right of return of the Palestinian refugees, and other resolutions passed over the years. If the Palestinians declare an "end of conflict" and sign a final

Tanya Reinhart

agreement as Barak demanded, then, formally, it is this new agreement that will be legally binding in the future, and previous UN resolutions will be nullified.

Further information gathered from three recent books published by Israeli politicians involved in the negotiations—Gil'ad Sher, Shlomo Ben-Ami, and Yossi Beilin—reveal that Barak specifically demanded that the new agreement legally replace UN Resolution 242. In a review of these books in *Le Monde Diplomatique*, Amnon Kapeliouk briefly summarizes this point:

> The Palestinians took care to base all negotiations with Israel on Resolution 242...This was the reason for Barak's declared intention of bypassing this resolution by turning the agreement he wanted to sign with the Palestinians into "an agreed-upon interpretation of 242" (Sher, p 21). Ben-Ami proposed transforming "the Clinton parameters"...into a special Security Council resolution that would be defined as an accepted translation of 242 (Ben-Ami, p 345). Beilin is the only one of the three writers who comes out against this trickiness. He criticizes Barak's foolish attempt several months before the Camp David summit to stipulate that Resolution 242 does not apply to the border between Israel and the Palestinians. These statements, writes Beilin "...aggravated the distrust before and during the Camp David talks" (p 249).[18]

Beilin, in an article from November 2001, emphasized further this difference between the original Beilin-Abu Mazen understandings and what Barak tried to force in Camp David: "The understandings did not include an explicit declaration of the end of the conflict, although that was implicit in their content." Beilin also argues that contrary to standard claims, "the Beilin–Abu Mazen understandings were never proposed by Israel.... On May 19, 2000, during Ehud Barak's term as prime minister, two months before the Camp David summit, Sandy Berger, the national security adviser for President Bill Clinton, visited Israel and met with Abu Mazen and with me in order to discuss the 1995 understandings." Based on Berger's conclusions, "Clinton accepted the proposal and wanted to put forward the understandings at the opening of the summit meeting at Camp David. Barak objected vehemently and insisted on an explicit reference to the end of the conflict."[19]

Under the conditions that Barak put for the final agreement, an end of conflict declaration was not something that Arafat could have accepted, nor something he could have concealed from his people.

Coverage of the conflicts that emerged during and after the Camp David negotiations focused primarily on symbolic issues—the holy sites in Jerusalem and the right of return. But the debates surrounding these issues only mask the real problem: that in concrete matters of land and resources, Barak offered nothing at Camp David, except the preservation of the existing state of affairs. Let us review, then, the details of his offer, as revealed in the Israeli media.

THE CENTRAL SETTLEMENT BLOCS

The only undisputed fact about Barak's offers at Camp David is that he proposed that the big settlement blocs—in which 150,000 of the settlers are concentrated—be annexed to Israel in the final agreement. In the Beilin–Abu Mazen plan, only the settlements themselves were to be annexed to Israel, achieved by drawing up a rather winding map that surrounds these settlements but includes no land on which Palestinians are living. Israel's strategy in doing it this way was to avoid the need of giving any Palestinians Israeli citizenship, and thus any accompanying social rights such as health care, or the right to vote. That, however, was not good enough for Barak, who "straightened" the maps, thus expanding the areas to be annexed. The annexation proposed at Camp David also includes the areas between the settlements, containing approximately 120,000 Palestinian residents.[20] Barak's solution to the "citizenship problem" was not Israeli citizenship, since "they will vote for the Palestinian state."[21] This enables annexing of the land without giving any rights to the annexed Palestinian residents.

One myth repeated over and over is that Barak, whose campaign promises included a "unified Jerusalem as the capital of Israel for ever," agreed at Camp David to divide Jerusalem. This belief is shared by both right- and left-wing Israel, and was the center of many political storms and right-wing demonstrations. In fact, there is not a grain of truth to this contention.

When one hears "the division of Jerusalem," the idea that comes to mind is that East Jerusalem—the part of Jerusalem that was conquered by Israel in the 1967 war—will be Palestinian, and will serve as the capital of the future Palestinian state. Or at least those areas of East Jerusalem still populated by Palestinians will be Palestinian. East Jerusalem has always been the center of Palestinian society, not just because of its religious and symbolic status, which is so emphasized, but also because it sits at the juncture connecting the different regions of the West Bank. East Jerusalem hosts many Palestinian institutions. Along with the famous Orient House, there are myriad welfare and research organizations dealing with health, water, housing, culture, and ecology. The infrastructure for a functioning capital already existed there, and many believed, following the solemn promises of Oslo, that it would indeed develop into such.

However, it is not East Jerusalem that Israel offered as the Palestinian capital. Let us look again at the clause about Jerusalem in the summary of the Beilin–Abu Mazen plan, cited above: "Israel will recognize that the [portion of the] area defined as 'Al-Quds' prior to the six days war which exceeds the area annexed to Israel in 1967 will be the capital of the Palestinian state...." This whole formulation rests on a verbal trick. The municipal borders of Jerusalem, under Jordanian rule, were broader on the southeast side than the municipal borders defined by Israel when it annexed East Jerusalem. They also included the village Abu-Dis and two neighboring villages. It is in fact this neighboring village of Abu-Dis that is designed in the Beilin–Abu Mazen plan to serve as the capital of the Palestinian state. The verbal trick was that Abu-Dis would be named Al-Quds—the Arab name of Jerusalem, meaning "the holy city." It is only through this deceptive use of definitions that Israel can claim that it proposes that the city be divided into the Jewish part, "Jerusalem," and the Palestinian part, "Al-Quds."

In fact, this part of the Beilin–Abu Mazen understandings has been long accepted by all parties. Behind the smoke screen of declarations regarding the liberation of Jerusalem, Arafat had already expressed his agreement with the Israeli position. For example, Akiva Eldar of *Ha'aretz* reported as early as 1998 that "Yasser Arafat accepts the idea that the capital of the Palestinian state will be Abu-Dis, neighboring Jerusalem, and sees the understandings included in the Beilin–Abu Mazen agreement as a realistic option for the final agreement with Israel.... In a meeting with the Middle East section of the Foreign Affairs Council whose center is in New York...Arafat was asked if it is possible to reach an agreement with Israel also on the question of Jerusalem. Arafat: 'Certainly, it is possible to accept the idea of Abu-Dis, which belonged to Al-Quds also under Jordanian rule.'"[22]

All previous Israeli governments agreed that Abu-Dis would be Palestinian, and would serve in the future as the capital of the Palestinian entity (which some agreed to call a state, and others did not).[23] Israel's condition was that Palestinian institutions would move from East Jerusalem to Abu-Dis. The Palestinians were authorized to build their future parliament house and government offices there, and these buildings were essentially completed long before Camp David. Here is a May 2000 report, from the *Independent* (UK), on the realities of Abu-Dis:

> "Palestinian Authority: Economics Studies Centre," reads the grimy Arabic sign high on the wall of the imposing new [parliament] building rising on a rocky, ragged hillside in the West Bank village of Abu Dis.... Abu Dis is one of three neighboring Arab villages that the Israeli Prime Minister, Ehud Barak, is planning to deliver to full Palestinian self-rule as a "down payment" towards a Palestinian state. Optimistic Israelis suggest that Mr. Arafat could call it Al Quds (Arabic for Jerusalem) and establish his capital there.... So, the spin goes, Palestine would have its capital in Al Quds, as Mr. Arafat promises his people daily, and Israel would retain Jerusalem as the 'eternal, undi-

vided capital of the Jewish people.' Except that, as Othman Muhamad Qurei, the 72-year-old mukhtar (village headman), explains: "We are proud that we are going to have a parliament here, but we are not proud that they say this is Jerusalem. Abu Dis is a suburban village," he says, "Jerusalem is where you go if you want to buy shoes."[24]

The Palestinians believed that Abu-Dis and its neighboring village Al-Azaria were to be included in the "second redeployment" that was agreed upon in Sharm-A-Sheich in September 1999, namely that they would be transferred into full Palestinian control (area A). "For six months I am being promised that I will get Abu-Dis, and nothing happens," Arafat complained in May 2000.[25] However, Barak kept denying that, and refused the transfer. On the eve of Camp David, Barak announced that he was willing to transfer Abu-Dis and two neighboring villages "as a gesture before the summit,"[26] but still he reneged. This is confirmed in Hussein Agha and Robert Malley's report in the *New York Review of Books* (quoted above): "When Barak reneged on his commitment to transfer the three Jerusalem villages to the Palestinians—a commitment the Prime Minister had specifically authorized Clinton to convey, in the President's name, to Arafat—Clinton was furious. As he put it, this was the first time that he had been made out to be a 'false prophet.'"[27]

In retrospect, it is clear why Barak withheld the transfer. He strove to make the fulfillment of an old obligation a central part of his new peace deal, in return for which the Palestinians would declare an end of conflict, renouncing previous claims and UN resolutions. Dragging out old commitments and presenting them as gigantic new breakthroughs has been Israel's consistent policy since Oslo.

In any case, the big "historical concession" behind Barak's willingness to "divide Jerusalem" is nothing but willingness to consider implementation of the long-standing Israeli commitment regarding Abu-Dis using the verbal trick offered in the Beilin–Abu Mazen plan. Let us look at one example of how this "historical breakthrough" was reported in the Israeli media. The *Jerusalem Post* of July 27, 2000, announced in its main headline: "Source: Barak was ready to divide Jerusalem." In the body of the text, we find the following: "Prime Minister Ehud Barak, at the end of the Camp David summit, had been willing to consider the possibility of creating a Palestinian 'Al-Quds' beside the Jewish capital, effectively dividing Jerusalem, a senior official aboard his return flight confirmed yesterday." In spelling out this far-reaching concession, the text adds that the proposal involves "allowing several neighborhoods outside Jerusalem's eastern border to be annexed to the future Palestinian state." The willingness to call "neighborhoods outside Jerusalem's eastern border" Al Quds equals willingness to divide Jerusalem. That's how it went every day in every paper in Israel and in the Western world. That's how a myth becomes accepted as fact.

As for the real issue of East Jerusalem, Barak had not

moved an inch since he pledged that Jerusalem would remain "the unified capital of Israel forever." East Jerusalem was annexed by Israel shortly after its occupation in 1967 (reaffirmed in a Knesset resolution in 1980), and ever since then Israel has been appropriating land and building new settlements there. All Israeli governments have declared that this is not negotiable, and that East Jerusalem will remain Israeli. Over the years, various plans commissioned by the different governments have been prepared for future arrangements for the Palestinian residents of East Jerusalem. Though they differ in some details, they are all based on the assumption that the sovereignty in Jerusalem will remain Israeli, but the Palestinian neighborhoods will retain some sort of municipal control—what Beilin called "an arrangement which is less than a municipality level."[28]

In the creative spirit that has flourished since Oslo, the Israelis are attempting to find language that would make it look as if the Palestinians have more control in their quarters than just restricted control over municipal affairs, control that does not even include the power to authorize the construction of new buildings. An example of this issue is seen in the following Reuters story:

A senior Israeli official said Tuesday that diplomatic language was the key to resolving the Jerusalem dispute blocking an end to 52 years of conflict with the Palestinians: Justice Minister

Yossi Beilin, an architect of Israel's seven-year-old talks with the Palestine Liberation Organization, said the sides were looking for constructive language for narrowing the differences. "The main point is what to call the status quo because everyone knows there will be no real change in the status quo," Beilin told Israel's Army Radio.[29]

"Autonomy" and "authority" were some of the favorite terms. The *Jerusalem Post* article cited above concludes its announcement of Barak's willingness to divide Jerusalem with the statement that the proposal "also included giving Arafat far-reaching administrative authority in most of Jerusalem's Arab neighborhoods."[30]

In an article analyzing the details of the Israeli positions in preparation for the summit, the very well-briefed Akiva Eldar[31] defined the position regarding East Jerusalem as "maintaining the existing sovereignty status, and allowing a municipal autonomy to the Arab neighborhoods, subordinate to a higher joint Palestinian-Israeli municipality." He further specified that "Israel agrees that Palestine will provide education, health, welfare, and even apply its juridic system to the 200,000 Arabs in Jerusalem." This illustrates the same concept that Barak proposed to apply to the Palestinians living in areas to be annexed by Israel: that the responsibility for Palestinian welfare and health will remain Palestinian. Although the Palestinian residents of the annexed East Jerusalem are formally Israeli citizens and their land will remain under Israeli sovereignty in the Camp David proposal, Israel will be exempt from providing them any welfare or social services.

The U.S. team at Camp David and later negotiations was viewed publicly as a tough group of moderators who tried to force both sides into more concessions. In fact, the U.S. position on Jerusalem corresponded precisely to the Israeli positions as outlined above. "The Israeli side, according to Sher's briefing, agreed to the ideas presented by Clinton in the final stages of the Camp David summit.... Clinton proposed that the [Palestinian] neighborhoods that encompass the city [i.e., Abu-Dis] be turned over to full Palestinian sovereignty. This would be done in return for the annexation of 11 Israeli settlement blocs, including Ma'ale Adumim, Givat Ze'ev and the Etzion Bloc [to Israel]." As for the rest of the Palestinian areas in Jerusalem and the Old City, the proposal was that the Palestinians receive "autonomous control over the Moslem, Christian and Armenian quarters...."[32] Recall that "autonomous control" is one of the creative names invented over the years to describe the Palestinian management of municipal affairs in its quarters.

It is hard to understand how so many have swallowed the story about Barak's willingness to divide Jerusalem. The facts about Israeli proposals were amply available in the Israeli press (I cited only a minute sample here). But they were packaged with huge headlines about Barak's unprecedented new vision, and apparently this is sufficient to shape people's perception of reality.

THE REST OF THE WEST BANK AND GAZA

The biggest fraud of Barak's plan, which did not receive any attention in public debate, was the fate of the Gaza Strip and of the rest of the West Bank—the 90 percent that was supposedly designated to belong to the "Palestinian state" after Israel annexed the big settlement blocs. The real question here is the fate of the settlements in these areas. Recall that approximately one-third of the Gaza Strip is occupied by six thousand Israeli settlers, including the military bases and bypass roads needed to protect them, and that one million Palestinians are squeezed into the other two thirds. Similar proportions are also found in the "90 percent" residue of the West Bank. The remaining settlements dotted outside the big settlement blocs in these areas were purposely built over the years in the midst of the Palestinian population to enable future Israeli control of these areas.

As a result, two million Palestinians in the West Bank are crowded into four isolated enclaves that together consist of about 50 percent of the West Bank's land, and the other 40 percent are blocked by the defense array of some 40,000 settlers. The lands surrounding the settlements were confiscated during the occupation years as Israeli "state lands." These include not only the settlements themselves, but also the hills surrounding them, some of which are occupied by a single settler's caravan. As in Gaza, large areas were confiscated

West Bank Final Status Map
Presented by Israel - May 2000

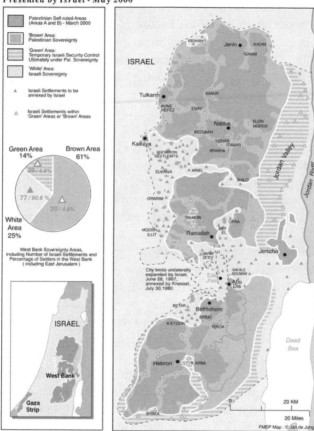

© Jan de Yong and the Foundation for Middle East Peace.

to construct special bypass roads for the settlers, "security zones" surrounding these roads, and army posts for their protection. Other parts of the presumed "Palestinian state" are large military and "fire zone" areas, particularly in the Jordan Valley. Israel has made it clear that these will remain military areas, as required by "security needs."

To get a sense of the current situation in the West Bank, let us look at a map (page 43). This is the only map that Barak actually presented to the Palestinians. He did so in May 2000, as a proposal for the final agreement.[33] (Recall that the "generous Camp David offers" were not accompanied by maps or any other documentation.) First, the map reflects the fact that the West Bank is already divided into four completely isolated cantons, with no direct links to each other, or to Jordan. The white areas in the map contain the big settlement blocs, and are to be annexed to Israel, on this plan. The green areas (appearing here with stripes) are defined as "temporary Israeli security" areas, and the Palestinians will have no access to them. It is the brown areas that were presumably proposed for immediate Palestinian sovereignty. They consist of approximately 60 percent of the West Bank, not even close to the 90 percent claimed by the Israelis. (Presumably, in subsequent Israeli plans the white areas were reduced and the brown areas expanded, though no official maps exist to corroborate this.) The small map at the left [Jon watch for directional]reflects the future of the Palestinian state on this plan: five isolated cantons (including Gaza) inside Israel—with no external borders with any other country.

But the crucial point is to examine the situation inside the brown areas of supposed Palestinian sovereignty. The map also reflects the present situation in these areas: There are still approximately forty isolated Israeli settlements there (marked with white triangles). These settlements, and the roads surrounding them, further isolate the Palestinian areas into smaller enclaves, which are marked with a darker shade. In fact, before the current Intifada the Palestinians already controlled these darker areas of the map (areas A and B). If the Israeli settlements stay in these areas, the situation will remain as it is in this map, where the Palestinians control only the present areas A and B, which are together about 42 percent.

We already saw that in the Beilin–Abu Mazen plan no settlements will be dismantled; instead they will "stay under Palestinian sovereignty." The public perception was that Barak made a different offer, which includes dismantling those settlements that will not be formally annexed to Israel. But as in all other aspects of his proposal, this impression is based only on tricks of language. Consider the example of how Gil'ad Sher, an aide to Barak at Camp David described the offer: "Regarding the Gaza Strip, the parties agreed that the strip in its entirety would be handed over to the Palestinian State. The settlements there would be evacuated unless the settlers decided to live under Palestinian sovereignty."[34] It all sounds so promising. Who would pay attention to the last clause that leaves the ultimate choice to the settlers? Precisely the same option was offered to the isolated settlements in the West Bank.

Left to decide on their own, the settlers will stay, particularly since not one Israeli government has actually given them a choice. The policy since Oslo has been to refuse all requests of settlers to relocate with compensation for the property they leave behind. Shortly after Oslo, the nonideological settlers of the Dugit settlement in the Gaza Strip sat on strike in front of the Government House in Jerusalem demanding to leave with compensation. But Rabin said "Not now!" Thousands of others in the West Bank registered in an office that Parliament Member (PM) Hagai Merom opened for settlers wishing to relocate, but the government refused. Based on past experience, not only will the settlers stay, but the settlements will be expanded. And if the settlements stay, of course the Israeli army will stay as well to protect them, and thus the situation will remain as it is now—namely, the Palestinian "state" will consist of 42 percent of the West Bank.

Just as before, unofficial rumors were spread in the Israeli media that Israel intended to evacuate some settlements in the future, but these rumors were baseless. All relevant government offices clarified repeatedly that no plan was being prepared for the evacuation of even a single settlement. Thus, Aluf Benn of *Ha'aretz* reported that:

> According to a diplomatic source, the Barak government has not formulated a plan to evacuate iso-

lated settlements in the framework of a unilateral separation or an agreement with the Palestinians. "There is no list of settlements intended for evacuation," the source said, adding that only general models regarding the future of the settlements had been discussed. "They will remain, will be moved into the blocks or will be evacuated. The meanings of the various alternatives have been examined, but no map or evacuation plan [sic] have been drafted. No one dealt with a plan for physical evacuation and no one will take a chance on dealing with it. We dealt only with blocks that will be annexed to Israel," the senior source said.[35]

Israel's policy has always been that first the Palestinians need to prove that Israel's imposed arrangements work, and then "we will of course discuss and consider."

A simple gesture Israel could make, if it intended any real agreement, is to announce the scheduled dismantling of a single tiny settlement, say the four hundred settlers of Hebron who are ruining the life of an entire city. In February 1994, after Israeli settler Baruch Goldstein massacred Palestinian worshippers in a mosque near Hebron, eight ministers—a majority in the Israeli government—voted to evacuate the Hebron settlers, who then numbered less than two hundred. But Rabin said, "Not now!—such decisions should wait for the final agreement." But when the time for the final agreement had supposedly come, what Israel stated at Camp David, according to Gil'ad Sher,[36] was that "Israel wants to retain control of Hebron for a period of thirteen to fifteen years. The Jewish residents of the city would be removed some time during this period. Kiryat Arba would remain under Israeli sovereignty. Regarding the Cave of the Patriarchs, Israel wants to introduce religious arrangements there that would resemble those on the Temple Mount."[37]

Both Hebron and Kiryat Arba settlements are in the areas presumably designated to be moved to Palestinian "sovereignty," as they re outside the big settlement blocs that were to be annexed. Still, Kiryat Arba (included in the green area in the map discussed above) will stay Israeli forever, and the Palestinians will not have control over their holy sites even in the lands they presumably own. As for Hebron, it's the good old "not yet" tactic that the Israelis are using. The Palestinians are to trust that in thirteen to fifteen years, after the total number of settlers has tripled and a third generation of Israeli children has been born there, the conditions will be more ripe for the settlement to finally be evacuated.

Similar arrangements were proposed for the Jordan Valley. Along with the 10 percent that Israel wanted to annex, Israel stated that "12 additional percent of the land, in the Jordan valley, will remain under Israeli security control for ten to twenty years" (see again the green areas in the map).[38] In any case, Barak clarified on several occasions that the settlements in the Jordan Valley would not be dismantled. Thus, in a meeting with settlers from the Jordan Valley, "Barak told them that in any settlement [with the

Palestinians] Israel would maintain a 'security and community foothold in the area.'"[39]

The language trick underlying both the Beilin–Abu Mazen and Barak proposals is that while the situation stays as is, the language includes some sort of Palestinian declaration of sovereignty over the land that the Palestinian Authority can present as a victory. It will even be allowed to "declare a state." White South Africa, at the peak of apartheid, offered the same to the blacks in the Bantustans.[40] It even sought UN recognition of these Bantustans as independent states.

This means then, that if Israel annexes 10 percent of the West Bank, "leaving the Palestinian state with 90 percent of the land," 40 of the 90 percent of their "state" is land confiscated and fully controlled by Israel—areas in which Palestinians are not allowed to build, settle, farm, and, in the case of the large military areas in the Jordan Valley, even pass through.

These details correspond to an earlier Israeli plan that received more honest reporting in the Israeli media. Under the headline "A State for Annexation," the front page of the March 10, 2000, edition of *Ha'aretz* announced "the prime minister's 10-40-50 plan: 50 percent of the West Bank for the Palestinians, 40 percent under debate, and 10 percent to Israel." The plan includes a third redeployment that will increase area A—the autonomous area under the control of the Palestinian Authority—to about 50 percent of the West Bank. (As mentioned, areas A and B together comprised 42 percent of the West Bank at that time.) In this 50 percent of the land, the Palestinians will be allowed to declare a state. "The proposal will leave unresolved the status of about 40 percent of the West Bank, as well as Jerusalem and the right of return," said the *Ha'aretz* article. That is, in return for Arafat's consent to Israel's formal annexation of the entire center of the West Bank, Arafat would be allowed to declare a Palestinian state on 50 percent of the West Bank, and to sell to his people the idea that all the other issues are still being discussed.

That March Plan is, in fact, quite old; it is an extended version of the Alon plan—labeled since Oslo as the "Alon Plus" plan—which robs the Palestinians of half of the West Bank's land. It is precisely the same March Plan that Barak offered at Camp David, but with one crucial difference: No one in the Israeli power system believed that the Palestinians would willingly accept the Alon plan and surrender half of the West Bank, which is why Barak proposed first to leave the 40 percent undecided. But at Camp David, backed by the United States, he tried nevertheless to force this as the final agreement. As mentioned, he demanded that the Palestinians declare an "end of conflict," thus renouncing all past UN resolutions and future claims— nothing would remain open for even a pretense for future negotiations. At the same time, Barak prepared the Israeli army to strike against the Palestinians, in case they refused.

The myth of generous Israeli offers at Camp David, then, is nothing but a fraud perpetuated by propaganda. The

Palestinian negotiators contributed to the smoke screen around Israel's offers, as they always have. They do their best to hide from their people how little they have managed to gain after years of negotiation. The crisis with Israel's right wing on the eve of the Camp David summit contributed further to the false impression that Barak made an unprecedented offer. The fringe right wing *always* objects to plans that leave the Palestinians with any amount of land. In the eyes of the far right, "transfer" of the Palestinians off the land is the only solution. But other segments of the right wing were perhaps victims of the Camp David propaganda. When the headlines announced that Barak was willing to divide Jerusalem and give up 90 percent of the territories, how could they know it was a lie? In any case, right-wing fury always helps to substantiate the propaganda. Today the right wing is protesting about Sharon's "restraint" in oppressing the Palestinian uprising.

THE RIGHT OF RETURN

If we need to single out one issue in the Camp David negotiations that has really convinced the majority of Israelis that peace with the Palestinians is impossible, it is the issue of the Palestinian refugees' right of return. The Israeli perception, fed as usual by massive repetition of the theme in the media, was that now that the Palestinians were finally about to get their state, they also wanted to flood Israel with waves of returning Palestinian refugees, thus leading, in effect, to two Palestinian states. Let us therefore examine this problem.

Israel's birth was in sin. As was mentioned in the introduction, during the war of 1948, 730,000 Palestinians, more than half of the Palestinian population of 1,380,000 at the time, were driven off their homeland by the Israeli army.[41] This is an open wound that needs to be faced. It is obvious that ending the Israeli-Palestinian conflict requires resolving the issue of the Palestinian refugees.

Given natural population growth over more than fifty years, the present number of refugees is 3.7 million, as estimated by the United Nations Relief and Works Agency for Palestine Refugees in the Near East (UNRWA).[42] Other estimates are even higher. Most of the refugees are in various neighboring Middle Eastern countries, and many are still in refugee camps. Twenty-two percent of all Palestinian refugees are currently in the Gaza Strip. The international community long ago established their right to return to their homeland or receive compensation. Most notable in this respect is the UN General Assembly Resolution 194 of December 11, 1948. Article 11 of this resolution states that the General Assembly "Resolves that the refugees wishing to return to their homes and live at peace with their neighbors should be permitted to do so at the earliest practicable date, and that compensation should be paid for the property of those choosing not to return...."[43]

Given the option of compensation, it is not known how many of the refugees will actually wish to return after more than fifty years in exile. Nevertheless, it is clear that the principle of their right to return should be part of any future settlement. The question debated in the negotiations is the implementation of this principle. Let's examine the issue in a broader context.

Over the years, two views emerged for resolving the Israeli-Palestinian conflict. (I am talking here only about approaches based on recognizing the rights of both peoples, ignoring "Jewish only" and "Palestinian only" extremes.) One view is that Israel/Palestine should become one multi-ethnic state in which both peoples are citizens, with equal rights for all. The other is that in the historical land of Palestine two ethnically based states will be formed: Israel and Palestine. This second solution is the one that has gained the support of the majority of both peoples. The Israelis are perhaps expressing most loudly their preference for a Jewish-based state, but this second solution is also the preferred solution of the majority of the Palestinians. Even at the beginning of the present Intifada, polls showed that about 80 percent of the Palestinians still wanted a two-state solution. Although the first solution presents a deeper vision, it appears that the two peoples are not yet ready for it.

These two views also entail different conceptions regarding the implementation of the right to return. In the first view, the returning Palestinian refugees can settle anywhere on the land, including areas that are dominantly Jewish, just as Jewish immigrants can settle in areas that are dominantly Palestinian. (In both cases, this would be, of course, subject to practical considerations and human sensitivity.) But the second view—that of two states—entails that the majority of the Palestinian refugees choosing to return will settle in the Palestinian state, and that the majority of the Jewish settlers will leave the occupied territories and return to Israel.

Palestinian representatives have accepted this consequence of the two-state view for years now, at least implicitly. They considered it crucial that a number of Palestinian refugees would return to Israel proper, as part of Israel's recognition of its responsibility for the creation of the refugee problem and the principle of the right of return. However, it was understood that this number would be determined in consideration of Israel's sensitivities. Though no specific number was openly discussed, there has been ample information in both Palestinian and Israeli media about the principled readiness of the Palestinians to compromise. The Palestinians viewed the Oslo Accords of 1993 as an Israeli commitment to withdraw from the occupied territories within five years, at which point an independent Palestinian state would be formed in those territories. This newly formed Palestinian state would be free to absorb all refugees wishing to return (in addition to the smaller number returning to Israel). The others would be compensated for their suffering and the property they left behind. The assumption has been that along with Israel's contribution, there would be international assistance on this issue.

However, as the years passed by after Oslo, it became obvious that Israel did not intend to implement this commitment. The number of Israeli settlers doubled, along with the percentage of land appropriated by Israel. The situation on the ground left no space for absorbing Palestinian refugees in the future. Furthermore, as we just observed, all versions of Israel's proposals insist that even if a "final agreement" is signed, Israeli settlers will not be obliged to leave the Palestinian land.

The assumption since Oslo has been that the Palestinians are expected to keep all their commitments and concessions, while Israel is not only exempt from implementing its signed agreements, but at the same time can expand its hold on the occupied land. By the summer of 2000, grassroots Palestinian protest over this inequality began to peak. The sentiment in the streets, in the refugee camps, and in the Palestinian diaspora, was that the refugees' rights were being trampled through a process of endless negotiations and false promises, and that if Israel breached all of its commitments, the Palestinians should also return to their original demand that returning refugees can settle anywhere. They argued that if Jewish settlers can stay on Palestinian land, so should Palestinian refugees return to their homeland on Israeli soil, perhaps in the context of one multiethnic state. This protest translated into political platforms, with many organizations demanding immediate attention to the tragedy of the refugees.[44]

It was in this setting of increasing Palestinian protest that Barak demanded Arafat sign an "end of conflict" declaration that would entail that the Palestinians have no further demands regarding the right of return. Arafat was expected to tell his people that it was time to let go of forever the dream of returning to their original homeland. With what vision of a new page in history could Arafat possibly convince the Palestinians that this was the right thing to do at that time? First, let us examine what a hypothetical mainstream Israeli leader, genuinely interested in ending the conflict, could have proposed.

Central to all Israeli proposals has been the demand that the big settlement blocs in the center of the West Bank (with about 150,000 settlers) will be annexed to Israel. This is already a serious deviation from the basis—declared as agreed upon by both sides—that an end of conflict entails Israeli withdrawal to the June 1967 borders, as specified in UN Resolution 242, but the hypothetical Israeli leader could argue that the process that took place in these areas is no longer reversible. However, as a modest compensation for the Palestinian loss he would offer that at least an identical number of Palestinian refugees would be allowed to return to comparable areas of their choice in the state of Israel, areas as close as possible to where the Palestinian centers were before 1948. This would be a very modest and minimal offer, which provides compensation only for what Israel took from the Palestinians after 1967. Even with bigger numbers of returning Palestinian refugees, Israel would still maintain its Jewish majority. However, I am not talking here about what I believe is both right and possible, but about what a mainstream Israeli leader could have proposed.[45]

There are two levels to address when striving to solve the refugees' problem: the practical, which we have already touched upon, and the symbolic. The symbolic level involves "the narrative" of the refugee issue. An Israeli leader seeking reconciliation on the symbolic level would first recognize Israel's responsibility for creating the problem. Opening a new page in Israeli-Palestinian relations and initiating a process of healing first requires acknowledging the painful history.

Commenting on Israel's recognition of its role in the refugee situation, Uri Avneri, a leading Israeli peace activist, said:

> Such acknowledgement must be explicit. It must be acknowledged that the creation of the refugee problem was an outcome of the realization of the Zionist endeavor to achieve a Jewish national renaissance in this country. It must also be acknowledged that at least some of the refugees were driven from their home by force after the battle was already over, and that their return to their homes was denied. I can imagine a dramatic event: the President or Prime Minister of Israel solemnly apologizes to the Palestinians for the injustice inflicted upon them in the realization of the Zionist aims, at the same time he emphasizes that these aims were mainly directed towards national liberation and saving millions from the Jewish tragedy in Europe.

> I would go further and propose the setting up of a truth committee, composed of Israeli, Palestinian and international historians, in order to investigate the events of 1948 and 1967 and submit a comprehensive and agreed report that can become part of both Israeli and Palestinian school curriculum.[46]

An actual Israeli leader interested in ending the conflict has yet to materialize. It certainly was not Barak. Based on a detailed survey that appeared in *Ha'aretz* a year later,[47] let us just review briefly what he did offer.

On the practical level of implementing the right of return, Barak hardly offered anything: Regarding the return of Palestinians to Israel proper, Barak demanded to keep this issue to the "sole discretion" of Israel. He insisted that "the declaration of the termination of the Israeli-Palestinian conflict would not be dependent on the conclusion of the process of rehabilitating the refugees. At no stage of the negotiations did Israel agree to take in more than 10,000 refugees."[48]

Israel's core idea was that it would be the responsibility of the international community to solve the refugees' problem. "The idea was that the international community would contribute $20 billion over a period of 15 to 20 years to settle all the refugees' claims. The funds would be given as compensation to refugee households and as an aid grant to countries that would rehabilitate refugees. The refugees would be given three options: to settle in the Palestinian state, to remain where they were, or to immigrate to coun-

Tanya Reinhart

tries that would voluntarily open their gates to them, such as Canada, Australia and Norway."[49]

The Palestinians demanded that independent of the international funds, and prior to their establishment, Israel should offer its own, even symbolic, contribution to the restitution of lost Palestinian property. Negotiations regarding a possible amount have never taken place, as Israel objected to the mere idea.

Apart from suggesting the charity of the international community, the only commitment that Barak's "generous offer" seemed to include was the option mentioned in the quote—that those refugees wishing to return would be free to settle in the entity to be called the "Palestinian state." However, there is ample indication that Barak never intended to allow even that much. In separate discussions, Israel demanded full supervision of the borders of the "Palestinian state" with Egypt and Jordan, precisely to control any infiltration of "would-be immigrants." In Chapter X, we will see that the same demand was maintained in the later "Clinton parameters" and the Taba negotiations of January 2001.

We are left with the symbolic level of the narrative— whether or not Israel is willing to acknowledge responsibility for the refugee problem. Resolving this issue would be of no physical cost to Israel. The least Barak could offer, if he aimed for an "end of conflict," is this acknowledgment. Creating a spirit of reconciliation does not endanger any of the declared interests of Israel. Nevertheless, even this symbolic gesture was too much for Barak. He refused, and insisted instead on vague formulations that recognized Palestinian suffering, but not Israel's historical responsibility for it.

Based on these facts, the myths and illusions of Camp David are more transparent; one can only conclude that at Camp David Barak was neither aiming for reconciliation nor genuinely attempting to move closer to an end of conflict.

CHAPTER III

THE SYRIA PRECEDENT

The most plausible interpretation of Barak's Camp David move is that he initiated it with the intention that it fail, thus showing that the Palestinians are the rejectionist side. "I am the one who exposed Arafat's real face," Barak boasted months later. As difficult as it may be to accept that such a large-scale deception is possible, the fact of the matter is that the Camp David negotiations were not the first instance of Barak's mastery of schemes of deception. Precisely the same pattern occurred a few months earlier in the negotiations with Syria. The analogy is chilling.

"THE VISION OF PEACE"

In December 1999, President Clinton announced the renewal of peace talks between Israel and Syria. The feeling in Israel was that of being in a great historic moment. Optimistic messages dominated the Israeli media. The polls indicated that most Israelis agreed to a withdrawal from the Golan Heights in exchange for peace. Even three months later, when the language of imminent peace had changed into one of a "disappointment" with Syria, and the newspaper headlines announced that "support for withdrawal is decreasing," the public continued to support Israeli withdrawal from the Golan Heights. In a comprehensive poll that was conducted by Tel Aviv University's Yafeh Institute for Strategic Research, 60 percent of Israeli Jews supported a withdrawal from *all* of the Golan in exchange for peace with Syria.

How is it that despite the support of the majority of the Israelis, no agreement was realized?

This wasn't, of course, the first time that the Israeli-Syrian negotiations appeared to have entered high gear. The previous round, which began in 1994, seemed no less promising. On April 11, 1994, the main headline of *Ha'aretz* (one of many) announced: "Working Assumption—A Full Withdrawal from the Golan." The negotiations lasted nearly two years. Still, nothing moved. Then-Prime Minister Rabin insisted that the sides first discuss all the details of the security arrangements and demilitarization, and postpone the discussion of the extent of the withdrawal to a later stage. And so, after two years of negotiations, the committees were still discussing the position of the early warning system and managed to produce one unsigned "non-paper" that didn't mention the word "withdrawal," while Rabin continued to invest huge sums in development and construction on the Golan.

It appeared that Israel was planning on many more years of negotiations, but why? Apparently, a cold status quo had been maintained with Syria for years—Israel had been free to annex the Golan, and Syria would remain quiet. But in fact, it was clear that without peace, Syria would not lift a finger against Hizbollah, which was giving the Israeli army hell in Lebanon. Rabin discovered an alternative recipe: During the negotiations, Syria must restrain Hizbollah to prove the seriousness of its intentions. About a week after the beginning of the negotiations, Israeli media reported that "Syrian army units raided Hizbollah strongholds and confiscated weapons."[50]

During the two years of negotiations, there was relative quiet in Lebanon, and it appeared that it would be possible to impose on the Syrians the same tactics that Rabin had played on the Palestinians—endless negotiations during which the other side replaces the IDF (Israeli Defense Forces) in the police work of the occupation. But by 1996, Syria's president Hafez Assad was fed up, and he withdrew from the negotiations. Gradually, the IDF's disasters in Lebanon returned.

When negotiations started again in December 1999, the feeling was that this round of peace talks would be different. At the time it was thought that the agreement was "almost all done" and would be achieved through short negotiations. It seemed that things were moving ahead at a brisk pace. On December 16, 1999, the two sides met for a ceremony on the White House lawn and by January, they were engaged in intensive talks in Shepherdstown, West Virginia. Then everything stopped. There have been no negotiations since the closing of the Shepherdstown meeting on January 9, 2000. At the Clinton-Assad summit in Geneva on March 26, 2000, the death of the process was officially declared.

The formal explanation given for the failure of the talks was Assad's insistence on controlling a small strip of land on the shore of Lake Kinneret. But an examination of the formal documents and what appeared in the media reveals a completely different picture.

BARAK'S PEACE SPEECHES

It is interesting to examine the speeches that then-Prime Minister Barak delivered on "the new era of peace" with Syria, since he used precisely the same calculated strategy on the eve of the Camp David negotiations.

The basic assumption in the Israeli public's perception was that Israel would be willing to withdraw from all of the Golan Heights (excluding a small strip of land on the Kinneret shore). But what is the source of this assumption? Not Barak's speeches. He never said "withdrawal from the Golan" or "dismantling of settlements." Here is an example of the art of creating false perceptions: In the December 10, 1999, issue of *Yediot Aharonot*, the main headline announced; "Barak on the Golan Settlers: They Will Leave Their Homes after Fulfilling a Historic Mission." On page two, the exact quote from Barak's speech at the labor center meeting appears, and doesn't include one word about evacuation—it's only about the importance of the settlers.

> They built a home, vineyard and village, and if it weren't for their work, determination and moral stature it wouldn't have been possible to begin negotiations with Syria, and we would have been now without security and without the Golan. We are all deeply connected to the Golan's landscapes, to the settlement mission on the Golan, which was mostly done by people who were sent by our party. I say to the people of the Golan: we take your hand in appreciation for what you did.[51]

The only source for interpreting these words as willingness to withdraw is a sentence after the report of Barak's speech in that news piece: "Following the speech of the prime minister...a senior minister said, 'It's all over, they need to start evacuating.'"

Barak maintained the same vagueness when he left for the Shepherdstown discussions. At the airport, he announced, "I am leaving on a mission of the whole nation, to bring peace, and I am moved by the scope of the responsibility. This is where Anwar Sadat landed, and from here Menachem Begin departed to make peace with Egypt."[52] This is what was absorbed in the public's perception—the analogy between Barak's negotiations with Syria and the negotiations that led to the peace treaty with Egypt. But if we pay attention to the text, we will see that the only element these negotiations share is precisely what Barak says, namely that in both there were departures and landings at the Tel Aviv airport.

Here is the rest of his speech as quoted in the January 3, 2000, issue of *Yediot Aharonot:* "Nobody knows what the border line will be"—a position which he repeated throughout the Shepherdstown discussions—"but I did not hide that there is a painful price for an agreement, and we will not sign one for any price. We are going toward a difficult agreement, but one which is necessary to bring an end to the era of wars. I lost many friends on the Golan and this doesn't come easy to me. It hurts me a lot to talk about the Golan."[53] If you want, you can interpret this pain over talking about the Golan as willingness to give it up. But the only thing that Barak explicitly promises at the end of his speech is that "we will not sign an agreement which will not strengthen, in our opinion, the security of Israel." And he kept this promise—he signed no agreement.

THE SHEPHERDSTOWN DOCUMENT

Unlike the case of the Camp David negotiations, the Shepherdstown negotiations did generate a document. The U.S. mediators prepared a summary document—supposedly confidential—that outlined the positions of both sides. The

January 9, 2000, issue of *Al-Hayat*—an Arab-language newspaper—printed a summary of this document, based on Syrian sources. Israel denied the authenticity of the summary and exposed the full document to the media. It appeared in *Ha'aretz* and *Yediot Aharonot* on January 13, 2000. Comparing the Syrian summary published in *Al-Hayat* with the Israeli version is highly revealing.

By examining the Syrian version, it appears that peace was indeed reachable. First, it appears that the border dispute could be resolved. Israeli media have often claimed that the debate remaining between Israeli and Syrian negotiators concerned a small strip of land between the international border (Israel's position) and the border at the time of the 1967 war—the "June 4" line (Syria's position). The importance of this strip was its strategic location in the control over water sources. On this topic of controversy, the Syrian summary mentioned a significant clause of the document, which states that "Syria acknowledges that the June 4th line is not a border and is not drawn, and therefore is willing to cooperate in drawing the lines" (Section A: "Borders Committee) so these sections refer to parts of the document not excerpted here? It's confusing). Interpreters in Israel viewed this clause as signaling that Syria might be willing to compromise on this issue, and perhaps would agree to symbolic water gestures, as was the case in Israel's agreements with Jordan.

Another claimed area of dispute had been the nature of the peace relations. On this, Syria proposed "to constitute regular peace relations, as between two neighboring countries" (Section B: "The Normal Peace Relations Appendix). The reference is to the 1978 peace agreement between Israel and Egypt, as a result of which Israel withdrew from all the Egyptian territories it conquered in 1967 in exchange for "regular peace relations" that included diplomatic relations, economic ties, and free tourist movement.

As for the security concerns of Israel, Syria "welcomes the presence of international forces under the U.S. command in the Golan Heights" (Section C: "Security Arrangements"). Even more significant is what's behind the screen: Syria committed to enforce that Hizbollah would not operate against civilians in the Israeli north, and it had already passed a painful test. When the Israeli army bombarded a school in the Southern Lebanese village of Arab Salim, Syria prevented retaliations against Israeli civilians, retaliations that were permitted in case civilians were targeted in Southern Lebanon, according to the terms of the agreement reached between Israel and Hizbollah following the April 1996 "Grapes of Wrath" war.

There is no doubt that Syria's leak to *Al-Hayat* indicated its readiness for peace. However, the full version of this document reveals how far apart the two sides actually were from reaching agreement. (Unlike Syria, which published a summary, Israel published the full text of the document.)

During the Shepherdstown talks it was reported that Barak refused to commit himself to a borderline and, like Rabin before him, insisted that the borders issue only be discussed at the end of the negotiations. This position is confirmed in the document. All that the document says about the borderline is that "the location of the border line will be determined by taking security and other considerations into account..." (Section I).

Let us examine the relevant parts of the document.

SECTION I
Establishing Peace and Security in Recognized Borders

1. The state of war between Israel and Syria now ends and peace is established between them. The sides will maintain normal peace relations as defined in Section III.

2. The international, secure and recognized border between Israel (I) and Syria (S) is the border defined in Section II. The position of the border was agreed between the sides (S: based on the June 4, 1967 lines) (I: will be determined by taking security and other considerations into account, as well as other crucial considerations of both sides and their legal considerations). The state of Israel will (S: withdraw) (I: redeploy) all its military forces (S: and civilians) behind this border line according to the appendix to this agreement (S: from this point on, each side will exercise its full sovereignty on its side of the international border...).

SECTION II
The International Border
1. The international border between Israel and Syria is as appears in the maps in the appendix—this border is the permanent, secure, and recognized international border between Israel and Syria, and comes to replace any other border or boundary between them.[54]

The document is a draft that was prepared by the U.S. for a peace treaty. It outlines a general framework, but marks by parentheses the points on which Israel (I) and Syria (S) differ. On the borders issue, the document refers us to an unnumbered appendix. Meaning, an appendix that doesn't yet exist and which is to include the maps to be agreed upon. At this stage, Israel hasn't even offered a draft for the map yet, and only provided the general phrasing that I mentioned.

But what really reveals how little Barak was willing to give for peace is the meaning he gives to this mysterious borderline that will be determined at the end of negotiations: Throughout the whole document the Israeli version stresses that after the peace treaty there will be no "withdrawal" of the Israeli army, but only "redeployment of forces." The difference might appear to be semantic, but the experience of the Oslo accords, in which Israel committed only to redeployment, reveals its meaning: Withdrawal entails *complete* evacuation of military and civilian forces, including dismantling of settlements and shifting sovereignty. Redeployment only

Tanya Reinhart

means moving Israeli forces out of populated areas to new positions, thus perpetuating Israel's complete control and sovereignty over the occupied territory.

Indeed, Israel insisted only that military forces, not Israeli civilians, would be redeployed in the Golan Heights, while the Syrian version explicitly mentions withdrawal of both military and civilian forces. Thus the document reaffirms what had been previously reported in the Israeli media: Israel did not commit to the evacuation of a single settlement on the Golan. Another indication of Israel's intention to leave the settlements intact appears elsewhere in the document, where the Israeli side expresses concern about "the arrangements" regarding the Israeli settlers who will stay in the area:

SECTION III
Normal Peace Relations Appendix
Defines the agreed procedures for establishing and developing these relations (I: including the time frame for finalizing the necessary agreements and the arrangements for the inhabitants and the Israeli settlements in the areas from which the military forces will be moved according to section I) (S: ?).

As we can see, all that Israel was willing to commit itself to in this document was a meaningless redeployment that would leave the Israeli settlers and settlements in place. To remove all doubt, let's look again at Section I. Its last sentence was: "(S: from this point on, each side will exercise its full sovereignty on its side of the international border...)." The assumption that at the end of the process each side (including Syria) would exercise full sovereignty is stated only by Syria, with no Israeli approval. (Recall that points that were agreed upon were mentioned as the body of the text and not in a parenthesis attributing the position to one of the sides.) The only plausible interpretation is that Israel insisted that whatever line would eventually be declared as a "border," sovereignty over the Golan Heights would still remain Israeli. In the meantime, not only did construction on the Golan continue all through the negotiations, but just as the talks began, the Israeli government awarded the Golan priority A status , which gave it preference for development.[55]

After Israel published the full text of the document—which was supposed to remain confidential—the Syrians suddenly walked away from the negotiations. As U.S. special envoy to the Middle East Dennis Ross put it in an interview a year later, the leaking of the document "killed everything."[56]

How can this be explained? It is reasonable to believe that Assad knew in advance that Barak had no intention of offering him more than Rabin's concept of endless negotiations. This is why he wasn't enthusiastic about renewing the negotiations, and as was mentioned again and again in the Israeli and U.S. media, it took massive pressure just to bring him back to the negotiating table. In normal circumstances, the need for this pressure seems strange—he is offered all of the Golan Heights, Israeli withdrawal from Lebanon, and a water arrangement with Turkey, and yet he refuses to negotiate. Without threats and pressure Assad won't agree to have the Golan back. But assuming that all he was offered was to continue to fight Israel's war with Hizbollah in return for a Rabin-style peace show, it is understandable why pressure was necessary.

Assad gave in to the pressure because he was threatened not only with an intensification of the economic sanctions in the middle of a drought year, but also with a "Kosovo style" air war. Barak, at least, mentioned his Kosovo vision on several occasions. In July 1999 he said, "I am confident in entering agreements when the IDF is very strong, equipped with the most advanced systems in the world, the type which enabled in Kosovo, for the first time in history, to lead a war which will bring the surrender of a local dictator without one casualty on the attacker's side."[57] But this isn't only about words. All through the negotiations, the IDF staged extensive maneuvers on the Golan—maneuvers that simulated war with Syria. During the Shepherdstown meeting, it was disclosed that the IDF was carrying out its fifth maneuver in a series of exercises.[58] How would Israel have responded had Syria done the same thing during negotiations?

Prior to the publication of the formal Shepherdstown document, Assad could justify the continuation of the talks to his people by keeping a vague impression of progress. It is to maintain that impression that he ordered the publication of the optimistic interpretation of the document in *Al-Hayat*. But once the full document was leaked by Israel (and then published worldwide), even if its meaning didn't sink in to the Israeli public perception, it was no longer possible for the Syrians to pretend that they believed Barak was willing to genuinely move forward on the issue, and Assad decided to quit the talks.

THE GENEVA SUMMIT-THE FINAL BLOW

Clinton summoned Assad to a summit meeting in Geneva on March 26, 2000. Before they even met, the Israeli media went a long way to depict the negotiations as stuck due to Syrian stubbornness. In the March 24, 2000, edition of *Yediot Aharonot*, a large lettered headline for an article by Shimon Shiffer announced: "Clinton Will Tell Assad: It Is Your Turn to be Flexible." But in the article itself it said that American sources felt that their problem was that "Barak is not willing to give us clear answers regarding the withdrawal to the June 4, 1967 lines, as Assad demands. He prefers to wrap his position in vague statements about what his predecessors have committed to, commitments which he cannot erase, and we are left to interpret his hints and convey them to Damascus." Barak is quoted in this article as saying, "I will not give any political commitment to Assad before we know exactly what we will get in return." This is precisely what Barak later said to the United States and Arafat at Camp David.

Indeed, the summit failed. The public image was that the remaining dispute concerned a strip of about five hundred meters on the shore of Lake Kinneret that Israel demanded to keep and Assad refused. Israel—followed by most of the foreign media—perpetuated its line that Assad said "No" to peace by refusing to compromise on this issue. As they did later at Camp David, the Israelis topped this by stating that this was Assad's last chance to reach an agreement with Israel.

But alongside this version of events another one appeared, one which was reported by Robert Fisk in the British *Independent:*

> The two men held three hours of talks, through interpreters, at the Intercontinental Hotel in Geneva, with the Syrian leader patiently explaining he was not going to fall into the same "peace" trap as the Palestine Liberation Organization leader Yasser Arafat. He will not make peace with Israel before guaranteeing the return of all of the occupied Golan, captured by Israel in the 1967 Middle East war. Mr. Arafat signed a peace settlement, then failed to gain a majority of the occupied West Bank or a capital in Jerusalem.[59]

In this narrative, the disagreement was not at all over the disputed five hundred meters of the Kinneret shore. "It was conveyed on behalf of Assad that he is willing to compromise on the withdrawal line, and even to full Israeli control over the whole of the Kinneret shore, while continuing to negotiate water rights."[60] The dispute was rather over the model for peace. There are two such models in Israel's history, one with the Egyptians, and one with the Palestinians. In the Egyptian model, all stages of the withdrawal and guarantees were finalized before the treaty was signed (later discussions focused on issues of Palestinian autonomy). The withdrawal was set to spread out over three years, and only after two-thirds of Sinai was evacuated were embassies and diplomatic relations set up. In the Palestinian model, the Oslo agreement was signed with almost nothing agreed upon besides vague Israeli declarations of principled willingness to withdraw in some unspecified future. The Palestinians halted their uprising and struggle, but they got nothing of what Israel supposedly promised Arafat. What Barak offered to Assad was Arafat's I still think it's better to say the Palestinian model of peace—nothing concrete, which means preserving the situation as is.

As it had always done before, and as it did in the Camp David negotiations later, the United States fully backed Israel at each stage of negotiations with Syria. Was the U.S. team fully aware, at each given moment, of the full extent of Barak's intrigues? Hard to tell. Years before, in a memo which I turn to in the next chapter, Barak exposed his philosophy on such matters: Washington should "be dealt with through highly complex and delicate preliminary discussions, which will in no case reveal the full extent of our intentions." Robert Malley reports that "in an extraordinary moment at Camp David, when Barak retracted some of his

Tanya Reinhart

positions, the president [Clinton] confronted him, expressing all his accumulated frustrations. 'I can't go see Arafat with a retrenchment!.... This is not real. This is not serious. I went to Shepherdstown [for the Israeli-Syrian negotiations] and was told nothing by you for four days. I went to Geneva [for the summit with Assad] and felt like a wooden Indian doing your bidding. I will not let it happen here!'"[61] which, of course, he did nevertheless.

CHAPTER IV

BARAK'S VERSION OF SHARON

It is still difficult for many to believe that a deception of such magnitude is possible. Deceptions and false declarations have been the standard in the politics of the powerful, and certainly are in Israel's policy toward the Palestinians from the start. Still, it looks like it would take a sick mind to intentionally conceive and execute such a plot, the type found only in absurd conspiracy theories. For this reason, it may be useful to also examine the history of the personalities involved. Although history is not usually determined by the psychology of individual personalities alone in the case of Ehud Barak, his background is extremely revealing.

Barak and Ariel Sharon have always been perceived as political rivals—Sharon heading the right-wing Likud party, and Barak heading the Labor party, which declares itself the more moderate and peace-oriented of the two. But despite their competition for political power, they share a long history of cooperation and a common worldview.

On the eve of Israel's January 1999 elections (when Barak

was running for prime minister), a revealing document was leaked to Amir Oren of *Ha'aretz*—a private March 1982 memo from Barak to Sharon written during Israel's preparations to invade Lebanon. (The document was probably leaked by Sharon as part of the Likud election campaign—whose candidate at the time was Benjamin Netanyahu—against the Labor candidate Barak. Sharon's hope was that the content of the document would dissuade the peace-camp voters from voting for Barak, which did not happen.) When Barak did not deny the authenticity of the document, Amir Oren published its full details in the January 8, 1999, edition of *Ha'aretz*. In the memo Barak urges Sharon to widen the war to a full-scale strike on Syria, exposing along the way his perception of democracy. In Oren's words, the memo "reveals a dangerous facet of Barak's character: his willingness to take part in a scheme intended to mislead not only the enemy, but also Israel's citizens, soldiers and elected officials.... Barak's deep and abiding admiration for Ariel Sharon's military insights is another indication of his views; Barak and Sharon both belong to a line of political generals that started with Moshe Dayan."

As Oren reports, Barak's memo was written "while he was serving as head of the Israel Defense Forces (IDF) Planning Division. Barak was then 40, the youngest of the IDF's major-generals. He was also a favorite of Defense Minister Ariel Sharon, whose protectiveness toward Barak outweighed the animosity of then Chief-of-Staff Rafael Eitan."

Let us review just a few fragments of Oren's exposition of Barak's memo, as the text speaks for itself (italics added).

"At the moment," Barak admitted, "there is no national consensus for an operation against the Syrians, except where the terrorists are concerned—[an issue] which under certain circumstances, such as a multi-casualty terrorist strike or a Katyusha rocket attack on the Galilee, might lead to consensus...."

With this in mind, Major-General Barak recommended that "the necessary infrastructure and plans be prepared for a swift operation, 1967-style, against Syria, [an operation] that will develop through a rapid chain of events—a terrorist attack, a strike on terrorists or on the surface-to-air missiles—and a quick escalation, surprising the Syrians and the Americans but not ourselves, into a comprehensive strike against the Syrians." After the initial accomplishments were achieved, there would be "further destruction of Syrian forces by way of a very deep indirect approach through the Lebanon Valley or by breaking through the southern Golan Heights, if the opportunity presents itself due to the redeployment of Syrian reserves toward Damascus or Lebanon...."

Barak proposed deception on many levels, each directed at a different audience.... *Washington would be dealt with through "highly complex and delicate preliminary discussions, which will in no case reveal the full extent of our intentions...."*

Tanya Reinhart

Within four to six weeks, Barak promised, we can put together a plan [for preparing the operation] which will keep the entire system—including the internal Israeli one and the IDF in the dark about the possibility and intention of using it. *Initially, it would be "enough to have five or six officers know the full extent of the plan...."*

Barak further recommended that the plan be concealed from various political figures (the majority of ministers? the prime minister?), since "the entire matter is very grave and requires comprehensive consideration. Furthermore, in light of the problems inherent in the use of mass force for the purpose of effecting change [in the international situation], *it may be difficult to discuss [the operation] explicitly and while clearly identifying its goals even within the political echelon...."*

All these preparations would come to nothing if the PLO held back: The meal, of which it was only the appetizer, with Syria the main course, would not be served. *In that event, Barak suggested, it might be possible "in indirect ways to influence the forming of a chain [of events] leading to an anti-terrorist strike."*[62]

The document's exposure was received lightly in Israel, and it was dismissed as a case of Barak's youthful folly. As Oren himself concludes his article: "If a young major-general, eager to become chief-of-staff, cooperates with the follies of a defense minister, should he be considered unworthy of the state's highest civil office 15 years later? The answer is no, provided that Barak has been weaned of the childish illusion that political goals of this sort can be achieved through military means."[63]

The media and the voters cooperated with the soothing belief that Barak had changed and turned to the path of peace. The structure of the myth was all there and ready—it was formed during Rabin's rule, who was also believed to be such a convert to peace. Had Barak, indeed, changed?

Sharon's "vision" has been that no amount of land should ever be given up. "We won't ever leave the Golan Heights," he has said, let alone the West Bank and Gaza Strip. Barak—Sharon's disciple and former subordinate—was mentored on this vision. In 1993, as the army's chief-of-staff, Barak, like Sharon, was a vocal opponent of the Oslo agreements. But Barak also understood that this vision could no longer be achieved in Sharon's way. One of the lessons of Sharon's war in Lebanon was that it was no longer possible to drag the Israeli people into wars of choice. Unprecedented protest within Israel at the time, which continued throughout the years of the Israeli occupation of Southern Lebanon, made it clear that Israeli society was tired of war. Did Barak renounce Sharon's vision, or did he simply decide that another strategy needed to be found to fulfill it? While we have no way of knowing what Barak thought, we can examine how he acted.

As we saw, Barak launched two sweeping peace initiatives—one with Syria and one with the Palestinians. The official narrative surrounding both initiatives happened to be identical: No Israeli leader had ever offered such radical concessions as Barak had: Withdrawal from all the Golan Heights! 90 to 95 percent of the West Bank! Evacuation of settlements! But the outcome of both initiatives was the same—"there is no partner for peace." In this narrative, Assad, who was given everything already, was not willing to yield on one single issue. And Arafat rejected all offers without even a counterproposal. That's how it is with Arabs, explained the narrative: Whatever you give them, they always want more. Hence, Israel cannot get out of the Golan Heights, nor the Palestinian occupied territories. There is no choice but "to shake the dust" and prepare for a comprehensive war of self-defense against the Palestinians.

As for the northern front, Sharon rejected Barak's ideas in 1982, as he was still hoping to be able to create a "new order" in Lebanon. Since that failed, and the Israeli occupation of Southern Lebanon turned out to be more and more costly over the years, Sharon developed a new plan—Israel should withdraw unilaterally from Lebanon, thus achieving the world's recognition as the peaceful side. In the spirit of Barak's memo, Israel should then wait for some incident. Under the new circumstances, even the slightest incident will be viewed as a legitimate reason for Israel to launch a devastating attack against Lebanon and Syria.

It appears that Barak had one big achievement for which

the majority of Israeli society was enthusiastically thankful—
he withdrew the Israeli army from Lebanon. Nevertheless, his
real intentions for doing that remain a mystery. I quote from
a column I wrote in *Yediot Aharonot* at the time.

> But there are still a few puzzling questions [regard-
> ing the withdrawal from Lebanon]. A first wonder—
> how is it that the border line has not been fortified
> and prepared? For a year, the government and the
> army have been discussing the withdrawal from
> Lebanon and when the moment came, it turned out
> that all that was done so far is to approve the plans.
> In most areas, the work will take another year.[64] A
> second wonder—how is it that there was not even a
> slight bargaining attempt over the border line,
> which now passes in the middle of [kibbutz]
> Manara's water reserve? There was not even bar-
> gaining over areas which were probably held by
> Israel before 1978…. And a third wonder—how is it
> that the right-wing is not protesting? Sharon seems
> to be furiously attacking Barak. But over what? Over
> the fact that Barak didn't deliver harder "preventive
> blows" to Beirut before the withdrawal. As for the
> withdrawal itself (to this implausible and unprotect-
> ed border line)—Sharon is warmly supportive.
>
> It is actually easy to understand Sharon's stand.
> After all, he is the first who proposed, three years
> ago, a unilateral withdrawal from Lebanon. By his

plan, such a withdrawal will provide Israel with the support of the international community...[and enable eventually] returning to Lebanon under better conditions. Whoever plans to go back in will not argue over the exact border line and will not invest time and resources in fortifying this border for only a month or two.

But Sharon isn't the one conducting this withdrawal. It is Barak. Then, still, why wasn't the border fortified? There are two options: either there has been a very big goof-up, or Barak is executing, in practice, Sharon's plan. Under the first scenario, Barak is determined to achieve peace, which can explain goof-ups here and there. Although it is Barak who suggested in 1982, in a memo to Sharon, to extend the Lebanon war to a comprehensive war with Syria, he has come to his senses since then. In the second scenario, Barak is the same Barak. Perhaps he believes that it is still possible to realize Ben Gurion's vision according to which control of Southern Lebanon is crucial for the future of Israel. Indeed the [Israeli] public is tired of the price in casualties, but it will soon learn that without Lebanon there cannot be quiet in the north.... Then the spoiled public will learn that there is no choice—we have to go back to Lebanon. Yossi Sarid, at least, has been warning for months that the road of unilateral withdrawal is leading, in fact, back into Lebanon.

The problem is that we have no way to know what goes on in Barak's mind, because he doesn't share his plans with others. Democracy or not—Barak is known to be a person who takes [makes?] his decisions by himself.... At the security cabinet meeting last Monday, the cabinet authorized Barak "to open fire whenever he sees fit," without having to reconvene the cabinet. From that point on, our future depends on whether Barak has changed. Is it the same Barak who wrote Sharon in 1982 that it is possible to keep a very small number of confidants who "know the full extent of the plan"... Or it's a new Barak, a peace seeking democrat.[65]

Indeed, we cannot know what Barak planned, because an unexpected development interfered. On June 10, 2000, two weeks after Israel completed its withdrawal from Lebanon, Hafez Assad, who ruled in Syria for thirty years, died of a heart failure, and his son Bashir Assad took his place. If an Israeli attack on Syria was planned at the time, it had to be postponed, since there could be no international legitimization for attacking the son for the putative crimes of his father.

But one thing is clear: Barak insisted on keeping a small area of conflict—the Shaba Farms. This is a narrow fourteen-kilometer-long and two-kilometer-wide strip near Mount Dov that Israel insists belonged to Syria, and not to Lebanon, hence it would not withdraw from this strip. (Both Syria and Lebanon deny this and declare the area is Lebanese and should be returned to Lebanon.) Hizbollah continues, as might be expected, to fight over this strip of land, demanding its liberation from Israeli occupation. This remains a source of tension and potential incidents. The story now is that Hizbollah, and Syria backing it, continues to threaten Israeli existence, and a war with Syria may be inevitable. As we shall see in Chapter IX, the Sharon administration is currently talking openly about such a forthcoming war.

Barak's narrative still accompanies us day and night, like a mantra and shapes the collective perception of reality—Israel's generosity versus Arab rejectionism. It is frightening to observe how successful this narrative has been. Those who believed the lies about Barak's concessions despaired at the chance for peace. Since 1993 there has been a constant 60 percent majority in the polls supporting "land for peace," including dismantling of Israeli settlements. (As for the Golan Heights, we saw that in 1999, 60 percent of Jewish Israel supported dismantling *all* settlements there.) After Camp David and subsequent "negotiations," the support for peace with concessions dropped in the polls to 30 percent regarding both the Palestinian and Syrian fronts. Barak succeeded where Sharon had failed before—he convinced at least the middle third of Israelis that peace with the Arab world is impossible, and that the coming conflicts would be no-choice wars over Israel's very existence.

CHAPTER V

OCTOBER 2000–"THE SECOND HALF OF 1948"

A HOLY WAR

The present Palestinian uprising was triggered by Ariel Sharon's provocative September 28, 2000, visit to Haram al Sharif/Temple Mount in Jerusalem accompanied by hundreds of soldiers. But the ground for his provocation was laid long before.

The Temple Mount is one of the most sensitive areas in the Middle East, as it hosts sites sacred to both Jews and Muslims. For Jews, Temple Mount is the site of the first and the second temples. For Muslims, Haram al Sharif is the site from which the Prophet Mohammed ascended to heaven, and is considered the third holiest site of the world's Muslim community. Since the beginning of the eighth century, the area has been an active center of Muslim religious practice, and the same hill also hosts the Al-Aqsa mosque, founded in the year 715. Jewish religious practice centers around a neighboring site—the Wailing Wall, which Jews call the

Western Wall, a name incorrectly suggesting that it was once a part of the temple. (In fact, this wall was not part of the temple complex, but a retaining wall for a plaza that was above it.) Jewish religious orthodoxy actually forbids Jews from praying at the Temple Mount area, or from even entering the Mount's plaza. The deeper principle underlying the prohibition is that anything pertaining to the resurrection of the temple should be left to the coming Messiah.

The sensitivity of the site has been well acknowledged by all Israeli governments since its 1967 occupation. Since then, there has been a conscious attempt by the political system, in collaboration with the religious establishment, to downplay the religious importance of Temple Mount and its relevance to present-day Israel. Asaf Inbari has written an excellent survey of both the history of Temple Mount—with its pagan roots—and the way the Israeli political system has dealt with it since 1967.[66] He reports, for example, that shortly after the Temple Mount was conquered in 1967, the Israeli Parliament passed the "law of preservation of the holy sites" that confirmed Moshe Dayan's understandings with the Muslim authority (Wakf). At the Parliament meeting which approved this law, Zerah Werhaptig of the religious party Maf'dal "delivered a ceremonial speech, in which he quoted from 'Masekhet Kelim' in the Mishna: 'The land of Israel is blessed with ten measures of holiness; eight of them are in Jerusalem and in its center the Western [Wailing] Wall, which, according to our ancestors, the divine presence has never deserted.'" (Author's translation.)

Jerusalem's holy sites

1 Temple Mount The 35-acre compound is a profound symbol of the Jewish nation and the place where religious Jews believe redemption will take place when the Messiah arrives. The area is also deeply significant to the Palestinians and to Muslims around the world, who know it as Haram al-Sharif (the Noble Sanctuary)

2 Dome of the Rock Islamic tradition says that the Prophet Mohammad ascended to heaven on a winged horse from this spot

3 al-Aqsa Mosque The third holiest site in Islam after Mecca and Medina in Saudi Arabia

4 Western Wall A place of prayer and the main focus of Jewish prayer

5 Church of the Holy Sepulcher Christians believe the church marks the site where Jesus Christ was crucified and later resurrected

Imbari goes on to say:

Werhaptig knew that he was rewriting the original text. "Temple Mount" is what the Mishna says, not "the Western Wall." The Western [Wailing] Wall is not mentioned at all in the Mishna. And why should it be mentioned? It is just a wall; it is not on the Mount; it is near the Mount, just like the rest of the old city. But Werhaptig, just like the chief rabbis, was thinking quickly.... He knew that it was necessary to immediately find a substitute for

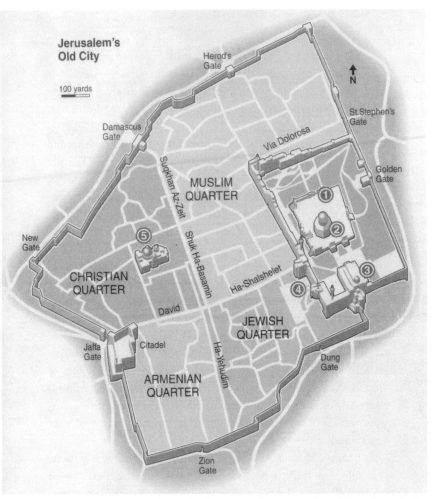

Source: Reuters, *The Israeli-Palestinian Conflict: Crisis in the Middle East* (Upper Saddle River, NJ: Prentice Hall, 2003). Reprinted by permission of the Palestinian Academic Society for the Study of International Affairs (www.passia.org).

Temple Mount, now that we [Israelis] control it, lest some Jews will want to build a temple on it or something of the sort. The substitute [the Western (Wailing) Wall] was there, ready and available, and all that was needed was to polish its glory....[67]

Throughout the years of the occupation, Israel maintained this policy of downplaying the importance of the Temple Mount. Only some fringe lunatics demanded Israeli control of the Mount. The messianic group Temple Mount Faithful was planning, indeed, a cornerstone setting for the third temple, but every time they tried to enter the place, Israeli police would be there to block their entrance or drag them out (as at the eve of the Jewish Sukkot holiday in 1990). Until recently, the words "Temple Mount" were perceived as belonging to the bizarre vocabulary of religious fanatics.

The first to change Israeli policy toward the site was the secular government headed by Barak, who made sovereignty over the site a major issue in the Camp David negotiations. All of a sudden, Temple Mount was "the holiest site of Judaism." Most vocal was the then-Police Minister Shlomo Ben-Ami—an ex-liberal who came to office from the university who declared day and night that "no nation can give up its sacred sites."

Israel's claim on "Temple Mount" is completely new, brought up only since Camp David. In the Beilin–Abu Mazen Plan for the final agreement—which was, as we saw, the basis for the negotiations—it was still stated that the area would be part of "extraterritorial Palestinian sovereignty."[68] Note that this whole issue is nothing but symbolic. As Jerusalem would stay under Israeli sovereignty and rule anyway, the only question has been how to guarantee some symbolic status to the Palestinians regarding the site. But Barak chose to make the issue a center of conflict. There was no way he could have been unaware that a new Israeli demand over the holiest Muslim site in the occupied territories was going to ignite further frustration and unrest.

In the last week of September 2000, Sharon, who was then the opposition Likud leader, announced that he intended to exercise his "elementary right" to visit "our holy site." This announcement was made just as frustration and protest were building up in the territories, as the Palestinians were realizing that, once again, they were not going to get anything out of the Camp David and subsequent negotiations, and that Israel had no intention of carrying out any of its Oslo commitments. Warning Israel of possible explosive consequences, the Palestinian Authority, along with Arab members of the Israeli Parliament, urged Barak not to authorize Sharon to visit the site. But Barak not only allowed it, he ordered a massive police and army presence to accompany Sharon and crush any sign of protest. There is no doubt that this provocation was coordinated between Barak and Sharon.

Sharon carried out his mission on September 28, 2000. A report by the Palestinian Human Rights Society (LAW) described the events of Sharon's visit as follows:

The visit was made at 7:45 in the morning. Sharon tried to make his way to the Al Marwani Mosque where an estimated 200 Palestinians squatted to deny him entry. Israeli occupation forces forced their way through by using batons and rifles. Among the squatters were Arab members of the Israeli Parliament, members of the Palestinian Legislative Council and a number of dignitaries and political activists.... The occupation forces failed to break through the human chain around the small mosque and managed to force Sharon and his team out of the premises. However, an estimated 1000 Israeli soldiers and policemen took to the roofs of the adjacent houses and shot rubber bullets and gas bombs at the peaceful protestors injuring 24 Palestinians.[69]

When these events triggered further demonstrations the next day (as could have been expected), Barak escalated the shooting and eventually ordered Israeli forces and tanks into densely populated Palestinian areas. At the end of three days of violence, thirty Palestinians and two Israelis were dead.[70] By all indications, it seems likely that the escalation of protest into armed clashes could have been prevented had the Israeli response been more restrained.

What is particularly astounding is how rapidly the situation escalated. In fact, almost every act of oppression or logistic plan that Israel has carried out against Palestinians during the current Intifada was already visible in October 2000. All the themes that presently define Israeli political discourse and propaganda were also shaped right at the start, during that month. It is revealing to examine the events of October 2000, particularly since no Palestinian terror attacks on Israeli civilians had yet taken place. (The first such attack inside Israel, during the present Palestinian uprising, was on November 2, 2000, when a bomb exploded in a Jerusalem market.) Israel defines its military acts as a necessary defense against terrorism, but, in fact, both these acts and Israel's propaganda themes were waged before terror started.

The Israeli army had been preparing itself for a clash long before October 2000. In June 2000, Barak informed the Israeli media that "there is a danger of Palestinian unrest, following the model of Southern Lebanon," and, parallel to the preparations for the Camp David negotiations, there was ample information in the Israeli press about the military preparations for a large-scale outburst, whose likely time was in September, "but the IDF was ordered to prepare as if it is happening tomorrow." If arms were to be used, "Israel will employ tanks and helicopters."[71]

Indeed, the full Israeli military arsenal was used right from the start of the uprising. By October 5, 2000, LAW was reporting that "Israel has used all means to suppress the protests, including the use of internationally banned arms against civilians such as: live bullets, high velocity bullets, dum-dum (mushrooming bullets), rubber-coated metal bullets, automatic guns, combat helicopters, tanks and armored vehicles, missiles (used against civilians), tear gas and rash gas, and rifles equipped with silencers used by snipers."[72]

In the present uprising—unlike the first Intifada—the Palestinians have resorted to using arms. But during its first days, shooting was only sporadic, and most of Israel's military arsenal was used against civilian demonstrators, funeral-goers, and stone-throwing crowds. Palestinian use of arms escalated gradually in response to Israel's escalation of armed oppression. By moving tanks and forces into densely populated areas, Israel provoked armed exchanges, and pushed more desperate people into a suicidal clash between unequal sides.

Unlike acts of terrorism against civilians, which all sane people denounce, international law and norms acknowledge the right of an occupied people to wage armed struggle against the occupying army. One can still question the wisdom of the decision to resort to arms. I believe that under the current circumstances of such unequal forces, the Palestinian use of arms verges on suicide. The easy way to exterminate a weak nation has always been to drag it into a hopeless war. A whole generation of Palestinian youth is dying out in a desperate confrontation within the prison walls, while most of Palestinian society—women, students, and ordinary civilians—are gradually excluded from the struggle. All they can do is wait in their besieged homes for the next collective punishment by the Israeli army.

Nevertheless, there can be no question as to the legitimacy of the Palestinian armed struggle. As the Israeli novelist David Grossman wrote in January 2002, in response to news of the seizure of a Palestinian ship attempting to smuggle arms to the occupied territories:

> What proof has been obtained here? Proof that if you oppress a people for 35 years, and humiliate its leaders, and harass its population, and do not give them a glimmer of hope, the members of this people will try to assert themselves in any way possible? And would any of us behave differently than the Palestinians have in such a situation? And did we behave any differently when for years we were under occupation and tyranny? Avshalom Feinberg and Yosef Lishansky set out for Cairo to bring money from there to the Nili underground so that the Jewish community in Palestine could assert itself against the Turks. The fighters of the Haganah, the Lehi and the Etzel underground movements collected and hid as many weapons as they could, and their splendid sliks (arms caches) are to this day a symbol of the fight for survival and the longing for liberty, as were the daring weapons acquisition missions during the British Mandate (which were defined by the British as acts of terror). When "we" did these

things, they were not terrorist in nature. They were legitimate actions of a people fighting for its life and liberty. When the Palestinians do them, they become "proof" of everything we have been so keen to prove for years now.[73]

In any case, even in the face of armed resistance, Israel's reaction has been grossly out of proportion. This fact was stressed in several resolutions by UN forums, and even by the General Assembly of the UN, which as early as October 26, 2000, condemned Israel's "excessive use of force" against Palestinian protesters, and called for the prevention of "illegal acts of violence by Israeli settlers." The United States and Israel, along with the Marshall Islands, Micronesia, Nauru, and Tuvalu (small Pacific states), cast the only negative votes.

On assignment for Amnesty International, David Holley, a British army veteran with field experience in Iraq and Bosnia, investigated clashes between the Israeli military and the Palestinians. *Ha'aretz* published an interview with him: "He related four threats posed by Palestinians to soldiers of the Israel Defense Forces and Israeli civilians: stones, Molotov cocktails, gunfire, and roadside bombs. He said that in most cases, Israeli soldiers would be able to rely on M-16 rifles and good intelligence work to cope with all of these threats. There is little justification, he charged, for the heavier forms of response which Israel has deployed, involving artillery and combat helicopters, among other things."[74]

Since October 6, 2000, Israel has imposed a complete "closure" of the West Bank and Gaza Strip. The Israeli army has prevented any movement in or out of the sealed areas. There have been reports of people going to work in the fields and getting shot on their way. "Every village and town has been cut off, making travel between regions impossible. The closure has gravely impacted health service delivery to Palestinians. Patients with serious injuries requiring referral to Jordan, Saudi Arabia, or Egypt for specialized care are unable to be transported. UPMRC's and other health organizations' medical teams are facing incredible difficulties reaching sick patients. The Primary Health Care system in Palestine has become paralyzed since doctors cannot access clinics and patients in rural areas cannot access city hospitals."[75]

Full closure and the imposition of curfews have since become standard, and have been viewed by Israeli society as normal and natural. As Amira Hass, the courageous journalist of *Ha'aretz*, described it: "How perfectly natural that 40,000 people should be subject to a total curfew for more than a month in the Old City of Hebron in order to protect the lives and well-being of 500 Jews. How perfectly natural that almost no Israeli mentions this fact or, for that matter, even knows about it. How perfectly natural that 34 schools attended by thousands of Palestinian children should be closed down for more than a month and their pupils imprisoned and suffocating day and night in their crowded homes, while the children of their neighbors—their Jewish neighbors, that is—are free to frolic as usual in the street among and with the Israeli soldiers stationed there. How perfectly natural that a Palestinian mother must beg and plead so that an Israeli soldier will allow her to sneak through the alleyways of the open-stall marketplace and obtain medication for her asthmatic children, or bread for her family."[76]

With the majority of Palestinians locked, defenseless, in their towns, the Israeli army was terrorizing selected areas with massive force. This continued throughout the U.S.-moderated Sharm-A-Sheich Israeli-Palestinian negotiations, and escalated on October 23, 2000, a day after the Arab League summit had ended. (The Israeli media described the period before the summit as one of self-imposed "restraint" to enable the Arab League to look aside.)

Under circumstances of returning gunfire, and often with no pretext of gunfire at all, residential Palestinian neighborhoods were bombarded almost every night from helicopters, tanks, missiles, machine guns, and "precision" weapons, while the Israeli army called on Palestinian residents to evacuate "for their own protection." Israeli settlers, on the other hand, have been free to attack, shoot people, and destroy property. Appropriation of land took place every day, bit by bit.

As early as October 2000, there seemed to have been a well-prepared list of places in the West Bank targeted for attack, places that Israel has kept returning to in the months since. The areas are mostly in the vicinity of Jerusalem or other settlement blocs—Beit Jala, Beit Sahour, Bethlehem, El Birreh, the south of Ramallah, Hebron, and several others. It is hard to avoid the conclusion that Israel has targeted these areas for a slow, forced evacuation that will eventual-

Tanya Reinhart

ly enable their annexation with the fewest possible Palestinians remaining.

Colonel Ra'anan Gissin, then Israel army spokesman, promised proudly that "Beit Jala, Beit Sahour and other [Palestinian] places will turn into Beirut."[77] And this has indeed become a reality for these peaceful, middle-class, cosmopolitan neighborhoods. Beit Jala is a striking case. This beautiful neighborhood is adjacent to the Jerusalem settlement of Gilo and its northwest side forms a corridor to the Israeli Gush-Ezion. Thus, it is a natural target for the land-greedy. The idea of taking over Beit Jala would have seemed inconceivable to Israelis just a few years ago. Its mostly wealthy Christian residents maintained good relations with their Israeli neighbors, and they do not fit the stereotype of the poor, invisible Palestinians whom the Israelis feel perfectly comfortable harassing. Despite this, Beit Jala was targeted right from the start.

The pretext for Israeli military action was a Palestinian shooting from Beit Jala into Gilo. Many Beit Jala residents believe that this shooting—at least in October—was an Israeli provocation. Yigal Sarena of *Yediot Aharonot* interviewed the Palestinian Tanzim (a youth militia arm of Fatah) commander of Bethlehem, who said, "We also caught collaborators of yours, who admitted that they shot, and we are trying to calm the situation. We won't give the Israelis the opportunity to destroy Beit Jala and kill the people. We will prevent it."[78] There is of course no way to confirm this, and the shooting from Beit Jala did continue for many months. However, it remains a mystery how the sophisticated and well-equipped Israeli army was not able to directly hit the Palestinian snipers. Instead, it had to bombard Beit Jala every night with shells, and turn its northwest quarter into a ghost town. As Sarena put it, "This week...I saw how this small tourist town turned into some kind of a small Sarajevo, a city at the beginning of its bloody journey towards destruction. There was, this week, one general who threatened to completely alter the topography of Beit Jala as if we were in Yugoslavia."[79]

The analogy to Yugoslavia was much in the air at the time. The way it was usually presented in Israeli discourse was as a hidden desire of the Palestinians to meet the same fate as Kosovo. In the tradition of blaming the victim, Israel claimed then—and continues to claim today—that Arafat wanted to bring destruction upon his people in order to gain international sympathy. As Amos Har'el wrote in *Ha'aretz:* "In Arafat's preferred scenario, the Israeli-Palestinian conflict would resemble Kosovo: increasing international involvement, foreign observers and troops, and finally an imposed settlement—which would be better for the Palestinians than what the Americans offered at Camp David. The minute parties other than the Americans are involved, Arafat profits."[80]

But the more realistic interpretation of Israeli fascination with the Kosovo analogy lies in the military option it opened of bombarding civilian areas with massive air force, backed by the support of the Western world. Aluf Benn, a senior analyst for *Ha'aretz*, described Barak's attitude during his July 1999 visit to the United States: "In all his meetings and appearances, Barak praised 'the astounding American victory in the Kosovo war.'" Asking "What is Barak looking for in Kosovo?" Benn answers that "one can conceive of a motive that will not be expressed openly, but it is, perhaps, most important within the political thinking of the Prime Minister: Legitimization of the use of military power to achieve political goals." In Benn's opinion, Kosovo's case appears to be the opposite of previous Israeli military acts. He wrote: "NATO attacked in the name of supreme moral principles, in order to return refugees and not to evacuate them. But in the 'Restore Hope' operation, there were all the ingredients that Barak likes so much: massive shelling and destruction of civil infrastructure in order to subdue a stubborn leader, and going out for a war which cannot be justified as self defense, but only as a pawn in the political game."[81] Israel has a long history of such shelling and destruction in Lebanon, but it did not receive the legitimization proven possible in Kosovo.

The Israeli air force produced detailed research (conducted by Amos Yadlin) of the lessons of the Kosovo war. Among its conclusions was that "the time available to the military force is a function of the political support and the support of public opinion at home. This support will be strengthened by immoral behavior of the enemy..." It also stresses the need "to be cautious about promising a 'clean war' with no damages to the surroundings [of the targets]."[82]

Indeed, by October 2000 the Israeli air force was already eager to try out such methods. Major General Dan Halutz, commander of the Israeli air force, threatened to "bring the weight of the air force down on the Palestinians if the current unrest escalates."[83] And he provided a detailed reasoning for deploying the air force against civilians. "'So far,' Halutz said, 'the risks of using the air force have not outweighed the benefits. No helicopters have been at risk.' He added that the IAF [Israeli Air Force] has no information that the Palestinians have shoulder-held anti-aircraft missiles."[84] The underlying reasoning appears to be that the only considerations before unleashing a massive bombardment of residential areas should be the potential risk to the Israeli air force, which was none, making the plan one of safe and clean slaughter—big benefits.

Halutz and his vision had to wait until May 18, 2001, when Sharon authorized Israeli F-16 fighter jets to attack "Palestinian Authority targets" in the West Bank city of Jenin, followed by other sporadic attacks. At that moment, the international climate was not yet ripe to launch the full capability of the air force, and there was a wave of reproach from the international community following the bombings. But "the support of public opinion at home" was guaranteed, if and when the military needed to use massive force. By December 2001—following a wave of brutal Palestinian terror attacks—the climate had changed, and the use of overwhelming force became acceptable. As the security analyst Alex Fishman explained: "Air activity with F-16 jets is per-

Tanya Reinhart

ceived already as routine. The commander of the Israeli air force, Major General Dan Halutz, has managed after a year and four months to convince the army and the political echelon that there is no difference between explosives coming down from the air and those used from the ground. Furthermore, the results obtained from the air are more reliable and effective. And not just Israel got convinced. The world has already gotten used to the picture of F-16 jets in the skies of Gaza and the West Bank."[85]

Since September 11, 2001, the Kosovo analogy has been replaced in Israeli discourse with the Afghanistan analogy. "If the United States can do this, why can't we?" is a repeated theme. Within a few hours of the attacks on New York and Washington, a top governmental and military forum that included Chief-of-Staff Shaul Mofaz, air force commander Halutz, and Deputy Chief-of-Staff Moshe Ya'alon demanded to "take advantage of the impacts of the event."[86] By October 2001, we had already heard that "the Prime Minister decided that the pattern of action that will lead to the toppling of the Palestinian Authority should be similar to the U.S. move against Afghanistan...The government's understanding is that the Western world will be more open to buy the elimination of the Palestinian Authority when it is packaged with current images and comparisons...Sharon hopes that the elimination of the Taliban and the elimination of the Palestinian Authority will be conceived as two parallel goals."[87]

Reference to Israel's 1948 War of Independence is the central analogy that emerged in October 2000, and it continues to dominate Israeli discourse and perception of the Palestinian uprising. The perverse Israeli self-image of the events, guided by massive propaganda, has been that it is the Israelis who are under siege, fighting for their independence, threatened by the Palestinian empire and the whole Arab world, just like in 1948. This line, which was initiated by the military, immediately found its way to the media, and has been repeated again and again by respectable mainstream commentators and analysts, like Ze'ev Schiff of *Ha'aretz.* "The Palestinians are using the same tactics as in '48," he explained in October 2000, and continued to elaborate on the analogy in the months that followed: "Palestinian Authority Chairman Yasser Arafat is doing everything possible to turn back the clock and to bring both the Palestinians and the Israelis to the initial stages of the 1948 War of Independence," he wrote.[88]

As the critical commentator of *Ha'aretz* Meron Benvenisti put it, the Israeli-Palestinian conflict is viewed in the Israeli discourse as "the unfinished business of the 1948 war."[89] Prime Minister Sharon stated this theme clearly in April 2001, "The War of Independence has not ended. No. 1948 was just one chapter. If you ask me whether the State of Israel is capable of defending itself today, I say yes, absolutely.... But are we living here securely? No. And therefore it is impossible to say that we have completed the work and that now we can rest on our laurels."[90]

But the current view of events as "the second half of 1948" was already formed in October 2000, particularly in the military circles. "The deputy chief of staff, Major General Moshe Ya'alon, the IDF's most vociferous disparager of Yasser Arafat, told his colleagues that this was Israel's most critical campaign against the Palestinians, including Israel's Arab population, since the 1948 war—for him, in fact, it is the second half of 1948."[91]

Ya'alon included the Israeli Arabs—Palestinians who remained in Israel after the 1948 war and became Israeli citizens—in the "critical campaign" Israel is facing in the "second half of 1948." Indeed, October 2000 also marked a dark turning point in Israel's relations with its Palestinian citizens.

Since September 2000, a well-orchestrated incitement against Israeli Palestinians began. A leading voice was Major Alik Ron, police commander of Israel's northern district. At a press conference on September 12, 2000, he announced that Palestinians from the town of Um al-Fahm near the Galilee—including "senior members of the Islamist movement"—had been arrested on "nationalistic charges" and arms smuggling. "This is the largest nationalist conspiracy uncovered in Israel since the 1980s," he declared.[92] Ron also accused Muhammad Barakeh—an Israeli Palestinian member of the Knesset (Israeli Parliament) and head of the Communist-led Ha'dash party (Democratic Front for Peace and Equality)—of "inciting" Palestinians to "attack the police." Two days later, it turned out that the arrests were on criminal rather than on "nationalistic" grounds, and those arrested were not related to the Islamist movement or to any political organization. But the press conference immediately ignited a firestorm of Israeli media attacks on Um al-Fahm and Israeli Palestinians, which continued after the true facts were revealed. Right-wing Israeli politicians began referring to Israel's Palestinian citizens as a "malignant growth" and calling on the government to indict PM Barakeh and ban the Islamist movement. This was followed by similar accusations against PM Azmi Bishara and PM Abdel Malik Dahamshe.

On October 1, 2000, a general strike was declared by Israeli Palestinians in solidarity with the Palestinians in the territories, and in protest over Israel's brutality. Images of twelve-year-old Muhammad al-Durra, who was killed by the Israeli military in Gaza the day before, were seen worldwide, and contributed to the sense of anger and mourning. There were massive demonstrations in most Israeli Palestinian areas, including roadblocks, and some stone-throwing. The police responded immediately with unprecedented force. As in the territories, the police overreaction only escalated the clashes. (In Shfar'am, where the police did not enter the village, the huge demonstration dispersed eventually with no damage to property or life.) At the end of the day, there were dozens wounded and one dead.

The next day, rather than seeking ways to calm the tension, the police escalated their measures of oppression. Meir

Tanya Reinhart

Yaron, who was commander of the police's Misgav sector in the Galilee at the time, testified to an inquiry committee (on June 14, 2001) that on the evening of October 1, 2000, the police changed their orders and, starting on October 2, began to implement the plan "Magic Tune," which enabled the use of more weapons, including live fire. (See Chapter VII.) In subsequent days, twelve more Israeli Palestinians were killed, and hundreds wounded—many in the eyes, victims of carefully aimed shots. The police brutality resembled that used by the army in the occupied territories, though there was no doubt whatsoever that the demonstrators were unarmed.

Some of the testimonies describing what happened during those four days in October 2000 are hair-raising. Asil Hassan Asleh, a seventeen-year-old from the village of Arabeh, was killed by live bullets shot into his neck from close range. *Yediot Aharonot* published his father's testimony:

> Asil was not a part of the demonstration. He was sitting about 40 meters away with his back to the policemen and was watching the demonstration. He thought the policemen couldn't see him. But suddenly three of the policemen started running towards him. I yelled to him to run. He got up and tried, but they were already on top of him. They hit him in the back with a gun, and he fell down. They continued to beat him. He yelled to me "Dad, Dad," but I didn't run. I was sure they would just arrest him. I didn't run, because I was afraid. Then

I saw them coming out from between the trees without my son. I yelled "Asil, Asil," and fainted. Then I found out that they shot him there.[93]

As in the case of the Palestinian uprising, the way that Israeli society perceived the events of October 2000 was as a threat to the mere existence of Israel. Aided by biased media coverage, many believed that the Israeli Palestinians had launched a war on Israel, trying again, as in 1948, to "throw the Jews to the sea." Angry mobs of Israeli Jews attacked Israeli Palestinians whom they encountered in the streets. On October 9, demonstrators chanting "Death to the Arabs" tried to burn a mosque in Tiberias, and others torched a famous restaurant in the Tel Aviv neighborhood Hatikva because it employed Israeli Palestinians. Similar incidents continued for days throughout the country. Needless to say, no Jewish demonstrator was killed or wounded in these riots. In their case, the police demonstrated a perfect mastery of restraint.

Thus, in October 2000, it seemed that all the seemingly dormant devils of racism were unleashed. Some gestures were later made to regain a form of coexistence, and an inquiry committee was created to investigate the events of October 13 (the Or Committee), but the hatred and fear these events generated have not died out. Israeli Jews started banning Israeli Palestinians' shops and business. They stopped visiting Palestinian towns. New mental walls were erected, separating neighborhoods that lived before, side by side, in relative friendship. Political persecution followed. Israeli Palestinian Parliament members have since lived under constant threats, and PM Azmi Bishara is already facing trial.

As in the case of the Palestinians in the occupied territories, the Israelis view themselves as the victims. The propaganda theme that formed public opinion was that the Israeli Palestinians joined their brothers in the occupied territories in their refusal to recognize the right of Israel to exist. The analogy to 1948, which most Israelis view as the Arab world's attempt to "throw them to the sea," has found open ears.

This analogy to 1948 is frightening. Official discourse defines "self-defense" as the shared ground for the analogy. However, the choice of the specific wording—"the second half of 1948"—could not have been completely accidental. The subtext it offers is that the solution too may have to be similar to that of 1948. As we saw, in 1948 the Israeli army drove hundreds of thousands of Palestinians out of their homes, and confined the rest to closed, restricted areas, governed for years by military rule. It is hard to avoid the interpretation that the leading military and political circles in Israel that produced this analogy still believe that "the second half"—a completion of the ethnic cleansing that started in 1948—is necessary and possible. In Chapter IX, I argue that this is indeed the case for large parts of Israeli leadership. But let us examine, first, the facts on the ground.

CHAPTER VI

THE FIRST YEAR: ISRAEL'S SLOW ETHNIC CLEANSING

THE POLICY OF INJURIES

To understand the extent of the daily Israeli crimes in suppressing the Palestinian uprising, we should look at personal injuries, not just at the rapidly growing number of dead. Again, let us look first at what happened in the first few weeks of the current uprising, since the same thing has been continuing, with varying degrees of intensity.[94]

On November 3, 2000, CNN reported a "relative calm" in the territories. Later that same day, there were 276 people injured,[95] and by the final count "up to 452 Palestinians were hurt [that day] across the territories, according to the Red Crescent."[96] On November 4, as the media covered at length Barak's "plea to Palestinian leader Yasser Arafat to return to the negotiating table and stop the Palestinian-Israeli bloodshed for the sake of peace,"[97] "another 153 were treated for injuries sustained in clashes with Israeli troops,"[98] including "5 school children from Sa'ir (near Hebron) who [were] in extremely critical condition."[99]

More than seven thousand Palestinians were reported injured in the first five weeks of the uprising, many in the head, legs, or knees by carefully aimed shots, and, increasingly, live ammunition.[100] Many will not recover, or will be disabled for life.

The pattern of injuries cannot be accidental. Dan Ephron, a *Boston Globe* correspondent in Jerusalem reported on the findings of the Physicians for Human Rights delegation: "American doctors who examined Israel's use of force in the West Bank and Gaza Strip have concluded that Israeli soldiers appeared to be deliberately targeting the heads and legs of Palestinian protestors, even in non-life-threatening situations."[101] Medical school doctors in the delegation explained that law enforcement officials worldwide are trained to aim at the chest in dangerous situations (since it is the largest target), and the fact that Palestinians were hit in the head and legs suggested that there was no life-threatening situation; thus, the soldiers had had ample time, and were deliberately trying to harm unarmed people.

In fact, the Israelis were not even trying to conceal their shooting policy. Interviews like the following one, from the *Jerusalem Post*, could be easily found in the Israeli media:

> "I shot two people...in their knees. It's supposed to break their bones and neutralize them but not kill them," says Sgt. Raz, a sharpshooter from the Nahshon battalion.
>
> "How did I feel? ...Well actually, I felt pretty sat-

isfied with myself," the 20-year-old soldier con-
fides. "I felt I could do what I was trained to do, and
it gave me a lot of self-confidence to think that if
we get into a real war situation I'd be able to defend
my comrades and myself."[102]

A common Israeli practice is to shoot a rubber-coated
metal bullet straight into a Palestinian's eye—a little game
played by well-trained soldiers that requires maximum precision. Reports of eye injuries are common. "On October 11,
2000, El Mizan Diagnostic Hospital in Hebron reported
treating 11 Palestinians for eye injuries, including 3 children. El Nasir Ophthalmic Hospital in Gaza has treated 16
people for eye injuries, including 13 children. Nine of them
lost one of their eyes."[103] "From September 29 to October
25, 2000, Jerusalem's St. John Eye Hospital treated 50
patients for eye-injuries."[104]

Stray bullets cannot precisely hit so many people in the
eyes, head, or knees. In fact, the Israeli army has carefully
trained for the present events: "Established just over a year
ago specifically to deal with unrest in the West Bank.... The
IDF has trained four battalions for low-intensity conflict,
and Nahshon is the one specializing in urban warfare. Its
troops train in mock Palestinian villages constructed on two
IDF bases."[105]

Specially trained Israeli units, then, shoot in a calculated
manner in order to cripple, while keeping the statistics of
Palestinians killed low. The *Jerusalem Post* article cited above

goes on to explain that "the overall IDF strategy is to deprive the Palestinians of the massive number of casualties the army maintains Palestinians want in order to win world support and consolidate their fight for independence. 'We are very much trying not to kill them...' says Lt.-Col. Yoram Loredo, commander and founder of the Nahshon battalion."[106]

The reason for this strategy is clear: Massive numbers of Palestinians killed every day cannot go unnoticed by even the most cooperative Western media and governments. Barak was explicit about this. "The prime minister said that were there not 140 Palestinian casualties at this point, but rather 400 or 1,000, this...would perhaps damage Israel a great deal."[107] Apparently, he believed that with a stable average of five casualties a day, Israel could continue "undamaged" in the media for many more months, as, in fact, it has. In a world so used to horrors, many feel that 140 dead in a month is sad and upsetting, but it is not yet an atrocity that the world should unite to stop. The "injured" are hardly reported; they "do not count" why quotes? in the dry statistics of tragedy.

Injuring Palestinians has remained a consistent Israeli policy. (By May 2001, there were already two hundred people treated for eye wounds at St. John Eye Hospital in Jerusalem alone.[108]) There are an untold number of reports describing the hopeless conditions of many of the injured, reports recounting the painstaking details of needs that cannot be met. A most acute need, for example, is physical rehabilitation. "For Gaza's population of 1 million, of whom 3,000 have been seriously injured in the Intifada, there are only two professionally trained rehabilitation specialists. Hundreds go without proper rehabilitation, not only because of inadequate facilities, but also because Israeli blockades around Gaza and the West Bank often cut off patients from health care."[109]

By December 2001, 25,000 injured Palestinians were reported, many of them blind, crippled, and maimed. Their fate is to die slowly, far away from the cameras—some because there are no hospitals to care for them, others because they cannot survive crippled amidst the near starvation and infrastructure destruction that is inflicted on their communities.

Israel's systematic policy of injuring Palestinians cannot be explained as self-defense, nor as a spontaneous reaction to terror. It is an act of ethnic cleansing—the process through which an ethnic group is driven from a land that another group wishes to control. In a place so closely observed by the world as Israel/Palestine, ethnic cleansing cannot be a sudden act of massive slaughter and land evacuation. Rather, it is a repetitive process by which people are slowly forced to perish or flee.

THE DESTRUCTION OF PALESTINIAN SOCIETY

During the period between October 2000 and December 2001, a clear picture emerged—beyond the countless details of daily brutality and cruelty—of a systematic Israeli effort

Tanya Reinhart

to break Palestinian society and destroy its infrastructures. A painfully precise summary was offered by Taher Masri—a Jordanian statesman of Palestinian descent—in an interview with *Newsweek* in December 2001. Masri explained that Israel has been working on three levels: The first level "is to destroy the economic infrastructure of the Palestinian territories, which are largely agricultural and, formerly, touristic. During the Israeli incursions into Bethlehem earlier this year, for instance, troops systematically trashed newly built tourist hotels." As part of this strategy, in large areas olive and citrus trees have been cut down or bulldozed. The second level is "to destroy the tools of the Palestinian Authority (PA), the police and security apparatus. At the same time that Sharon demands Arafat crack down on Hamas and Islamic Jihad, Israel has in recent months destroyed 80 per cent of the PA's police headquarters.... Sharon also places severe limits on the ability of the Palestinian Authority to send police reinforcements from one area to another." Thirdly, Masri says, "Sharon is eliminating—liquidating—the Palestinian leadership. He is hitting the third rank now, but he will move up to the first. Without leadership, without economic lifeblood, without security tools for the PA, the people will be ready to leave the country."[110]

During the four decades of occupation, Israel has enforced a total dependence of the Palestinian economy on Israel. The Oslo agreements deepened this dependence, and gave it a semi-legal status, following the model of the Bantustans in

South Africa. The economic agreement between Israel and the Palestinians speaks eloquently of the "normal passage of workers" between both sides, "notwithstanding the right of each side to redefine from time to time the scale and conditions of the entry of workers into their area." (For more on the economic agreements, see the Appendix.) In more mundane words, this means complete Israeli control over the Palestinian workforce. All other aspects of economy, like trade, were also left under strict Israeli control. This total control has enabled Israel to impose a full economic blockade on the territories from the outset of the uprising, completely blocking Palestinians from work in Israel and any Palestinian trade options.

The economic conditions of the Palestinians in the occupied territories, which deteriorated sharply during the Oslo years,[111] have reached a disastrous level during the months of the new uprising. Israel's siege has locked Palestinians in their hometowns and has meant a severe loss of employment and income. By December 2001, according to MIFTAH's (the Palestinian Initiative for the Promotion of Global Dialogue and Democracy) figures,[112] the unemployment rate in the West Bank and Gaza Strip was 57 percent. This includes not only those who lost their jobs in Israel, but also those who cannot travel to work because of the closures and roadblocks, as well as victims of businesses that collapsed or closed.[113]

Agriculture—which, as Masri points out, is a major income source—has suffered enormously. Israel's economic blockade of the territories has meant the loss of any possibility of exporting. As with the job market, the occupied territories depend on Israel for selling their products, either to Israel itself, or abroad. (Under the Oslo agreements, the Palestinians were not allowed to export directly, but only via Israeli export companies.) A document prepared by the Israeli Defense Force at the outset of the uprising explained—among the other economic measures the Palestinians were to expect—that "had violence not erupted, the Palestinian Authority would have constituted Israel's main source of agricultural products during the next year. Given the current situation...that produce [will] not be sold to Israel...which will import this produce from other countries, in order to meet demand."[114]

But by now, it is not even a matter of export anymore, but of mere survival. Israel shows no more compassion to the land than it does to the people. MIFTAH reports that by December 2001, the number of olive trees uprooted from Palestinian land was 112,900, and the area of cultivated Palestinian land destroyed was 3,669,000 square meters. On top of this, in many places farmers cannot get out to work or harvest their fields because of Israel's military siege.

Fifty-three percent of Palestinians are living below the poverty line, which means they live on less than two dollars a day. The proud and sophisticated Palestinian society is being forced into despair. Here is just one report from the British *Guardian:*

Before the intifada began last September, the number of Palestinians lining up for food sacks from the UN Relief and Works Agency for Palestine Refugees in the Near East (UNRWA) was relatively small, restricted to a few cases of hardship. Now a substantial majority queue for aid...An UNRWA official in Jerusalem said that food sacks were being distributed to about 217,000 families throughout the West Bank and Gaza. But shortage of funds, despite an international appeal, means such deliveries are restricted to three-month intervals...The food parcels are modest: comprising flour, lentils, sugar, cooking oil, dried milk, rice and 150 shekels [about $37.00]. But with many Palestinians unable to cross the blockade and travel to work, the handouts are a form of subsistence.

At Jalazun, north of Ramallah on the West Bank, the arrival of the UN vehicles also brings noisy confusion. With flour clouding the air, the sweating aid workers pass sack after sack from the back of lorries to the men, women and children waiting below. Press coverage of the convoys is discouraged because the recipients often feel humiliated: their attitude is that food aid is something for poor African countries, not for Palestinians...Among the women lining up was mother of six Nuriddin Kharoub, 46, who admitted feeling humiliated. "I am embarrassed. It is like begging," she says. "Who wants to be like a beggar?"[115]

Israel has been blocking supplies to the occupied territories, thus exacerbating Palestinian's economic collapse. By early November 2000, the *Independent* reported that: "More than 900 truckloads for Palestinian territories are stuck at the Israeli ports of Haifa and Ashdod. So are 1,000 new and used cars. At the same time, Israel is delaying the monthly transfer of about 30 shekels [approx. $7.50 at the time] in tax revenue paid by Palestinian workers or importers.... The Israelis do not deny wielding the economic weapon. 'We are not trying to starve them out,' said a government spokesman, 'but we are using any means to convince the Palestinians to stop the violence. There is a struggle going on, Palestinians versus Israelis, and Israel is entitled to take every measure to defend itself.'"[116]

This is confirmed by the IDF report quoted above, couched in the appropriate language of Israel's fight against terrorism, which, recall, at the time had not even started. "Furthermore, huge quantities of goods intended for the Palestinian Authority remain undelivered in the Israeli port of Ashdod. This is a result of the Palestinian demand that its security personnel be allowed through the Karni Passage into Israel, to take delivery of the goods, without undergoing any form of security check. Israel cannot allow such hazardous entry into its border, which would increase the risk of terror attacks on Israeli civilians, especially when it is known that Palestinian officials are involved in arms smuggling. Therefore the goods remain where they are."[117]

This policy, like everything else, has escalated with time. By December 2001, Amira Hass reported that it was "difficult to grasp all the information that comes from these besieged places. The lack of medical supplies, such as oxygen tanks, is a daily, desperate routine in the hospitals. Cooking gas and fuel and even drinking water routinely run out. Suppliers have difficulties bringing in fresh food."[118]

In the next chapter I will turn to Israel's efforts to destroy the institutions of the Palestinian Authority and the leadership of Arafat, efforts that have accompanied Israel's economic blockade. But first let us examine the third level of destruction—the assassinations and the liquidation of the Palestinian leadership.

Israel's policy of political assassination is not new; it has been employed for many years, both in the occupied territories and abroad, including during the Oslo years. But since the escalation of violence that began in October 2000, Israel's use of assassination has reached new levels: Death squad units operate daily, and Israel openly executes political and military leaders. As Masri pointed out, the political assassinations first targeted local leadership of the third or second rank, but they have been moving up. The most senior political leader assassinated (in August 2001) was Abu Ali Mustafa, head of the PFLP (Popular Front for the Liberation of Palestine), part of the coalition of the Palestinian Authority.

Originally, there was much criticism within Israeli society when the special units currently in charge of carrying out assassinations were formed during the previous Palestinian Intifada of the 1980's.[119] It was repeatedly pointed out that assassination meant bypassing the legal system. It was argued that even those who are indeed suspected of being dangerous terrorists have the right to be tried, to be given the chance to argue and present evidence in their own defense, and to refute the allegations against them. Not only are the people who are targeted for assassination deprived of any such legal rights, but there is also no legal or other means of supervising who is added to the target list as this is left to the discretion of the security services. Many describe these operations as "state terrorism," and for a long while they were kept secret because of Israeli public opinion.

Even in the current phase of violence and escalation, when hardly any criticism of the government or army is expressed in Israel, the Civil Rights Committee of the Israel Bar Association denounced, in December 2001, the government policy on "targeted assassinations" of Palestinians. "This is the first time a committee of the bar association has taken a strong stand and pointed out the inherent legal problem of 'execution without trial.'" The committee, chaired by attorney Yosi Arnon, stated, "This policy is illegal and against laws of war and international law that define liquidation as a serious war crime."[120]

As with everything else, Israel describes its assassination policy as part of its "war against terror." Everyone assassinated is declared a terrorist, a "ticking bomb," or a conspirator actively involved in the planning of acts of terror. While some of those assassinated were indeed likely involved in terror activities, many others were not. At the end of December 2000 a "step-up" in the assassination policy was declared, which also aims at political figures. The Israeli media disclosed this quite openly: *Ma'ariv* explained that "over the last few days Israel has adopted a more extreme attitude toward the Palestinian Authority. In this framework the IDF and the GSS [General Security Service –Shin Bet] have been given permission to raise the threshold of elimination operations so as to also include senior figures and Palestinian Authority officials."[121] *Yediot Aharonot* said that "a senior political-security source even intimated that this is a real step-up. It would mean not only applying economic pressure, retracting all the easing of restrictions, restricting movement and placing a severe closure on the Palestinians, but from now on Israel would escalate also its deterrent operations. The IDF and GSS would no longer stop at attacking the actual terror activists..."[122]

Among the political figures targeted following that step-up decision at the end of December 2000 was the renowned moderate leader Dr. Thabet Thabet. The *Ma'ariv* article cited above went on to report that "permission given by Prime Minister Ehud Barak is what enabled the killing of Dr. Thabet Thabet, the director general of the Fatah Movement in Tul Karem." Israel keeps insisting that the assassination was a "security-related operation." Thus, the *Ma'ariv* article also stated that "a senior security establishment official revealed yesterday that Thabet had been responsible for all of the Tanzim attacks in the Tul Karem sector." (The Tanzim is a youth militia of Arafat's Fatah organization headed by Marwan Barghuti.) But a completely different picture emerged from Peace Now[123] circles, as Yehudit Har'el, an Israeli peace activist, wrote on the day of Thabet's assassination:

> Dr Thabet Thabet was well known to many Israeli Peace Now activists. From the very beginning of the first Intifada, in 1988 he gave his blessing and was an active partner in many joint activities conducted by Palestinian and Israeli Peace activists. Later...Dr Thabet was a most influential partner of the Peace Now movement in organizing joint political activities as well as dialogue groups between Israelis and Palestinians during the Intifada, prior to Oslo and after the Oslo agreements. Dr Thabet was an influential political leader who believed wholeheartedly in the necessity of a historical compromise between the two peoples. Back in 1993 he was a staunch supporter of the Oslo agreements and he had a clear vision of peaceful coexistence between the two peoples in this land. In one of his public speeches he said: "We are two peoples but we have one future and we must learn to live together in peace in two independent states." Just two weeks ago he expressed his belief in the feasibility of Peace

on the basis of a Two State solution.... This morning Dr Thabet was brutally murdered by Israeli forces. He left behind a widow and two orphans. His blood is crying out from the earth where it was spilt by our hands! God bless his soul and forgive us for allowing these atrocities to happen.[124]

Most likely, the assassination of a moderate leader is a signal—both to the Palestinians and to the Israeli peace movement—that the days of "peace games" are over. In the project of ethnic cleansing, moderates pose the most dangerous threat, as they embody the alternative option of coexistence. As a "security source" said about Dr. Sari Nuseibbeh, a consistent Palestinian voice of moderation and peace, "because of his sophistication, he is much more dangerous, as far as we are concerned, than many other figures in the Palestinian leadership."[125]

The months of brutal oppression have had their toll. A slow process of migration has begun. Many of the wealthier and professional elites—those who could afford it—fled to Western countries. Israel encouraged this process and provided assistance to those able to leave. By October 2000, it was being reported that "since the outbreak of violence in the West Bank and Gaza Strip, hundreds of Christian Arab families have left with the assistance of the Foreign Ministry and foreign embassies."[126] By June 2001, more than 150,000 others had left for Jordan, which, alarmed by the danger of a more massive flux of refugees, started to close its border.[127] Forcing out a society's elites is a part of the process of ethnic cleansing, and makes the remaining population that much more vulnerable. Taher Masri, in the interview cited above, explains Israel's policy as follows: "Israeli Prime Minister Ariel Sharon's long-term plan is to force the Palestinians off the West Bank first into untenable enclaves, and eventually into exile."[128]

In December 2001, Dr. Mustafa Barghouthi, director of the Palestinian Health Development Information and Policy Institute,[129] issued a painful appeal to the world:

> The current situation in Palestine is verging on that of a humanitarian crisis. The Palestinian population—3.2 million people—is currently living under the worst siege in their entire history. People are unable to move between Palestinian villages and towns, and goods cannot be transported. Large parts of many cities and villages are under 24-hour, or dusk-to-dawn curfews; tanks and armored personal carriers sit in the streets, outside homes. A shortage of supplies is being reported in some areas, including gas and food. Sewage and garbage remains [sic] uncollected, presenting a public health crisis. Vaccinations and primary health care systems are paralyzed, and epidemics are possible. Patients in need of kidney dialysis and cancer treatment cannot receive it. 30 Palestinians died after being denied access to medical care, and numerous

women have given birth at the Israeli military blockades. Heavily armed Israeli soldiers arbitrarily occupy civilians' homes. Israeli soldiers make armed raids into areas under Palestinian Authority, shooting people in their homes, and arresting others. Without your actions the situation can only worsen.[130]

Dr. Barghouthi has been since beaten and detained several times by Israeli forces.

When this chapter was written, in December 2001, it seemed to me that we had already seen the worst—that going beyond the level of steady, daily ethnic cleansing that Barghouthi described was something the world would not let happen. But it turned out that those were humane times compared to what was to come next, a subject we will return to in Chapter VIII.

DECEMBER 2001: "TOPPLE ARAFAT"

In December 2001, Israel made official what had been in the air for many months before—that it had been aiming to eventually destroy the Palestinian Authority and Arafat's rule. The Oslo process, which enabled the construction of a limited Palestinian self-rule in parts of the occupied territories, was by then basically considered "a historical mistake." As Sharon declared in October 2001, "Oslo is not continuing; there won't be Oslo; Oslo is over."[131]

The Israeli cabinet decisions of December 3, 2001, followed a horrible Hamas terror attack on a bus in Haifa that killed thirty Israeli civilians. The attack coincided with Sharon's visit to the United States, and, according to the Israeli media, while there, Sharon obtained a "green light" from the U.S. for the new phase of eliminating the Palestinian Authority. The official bulletin of the special cabinet meeting states that "the Cabinet has determined that last weekend's deadly and cruel terror attacks illustrate our enemies' lack of inhibitions, and require actions more wide ranging than those taken against the Palestinian terrorism until now...the Government has determined that the Palestinian Authority is an entity that supports terrorism, and must be dealt with accordingly. In the framework of this decision, the Ministerial Committee for National Security is authorized to decide on operational steps (military, diplomatic, informational and economic).... The Israeli information campaign will focus on Arafat's responsibility for the terrorism emanating from the areas under his control."[132]

The "operational steps" followed immediately. F-16 jets were ordered to attack and destroy Palestinian institutions. The targets were not just police stations or Gaza's airport, but civilian institutions of the Palestinian Authority, including a television station. On December 5, 2001, the Israeli army raided the Palestinian Central Bureau of Statistics in Ramallah, destroying or confiscating computers and documents. As Edward Said wrote, they were "effacing virtually the entire record of collective Palestinian life. In 1982, the same army under the same commander entered West Beirut and carted off documents and files from the Palestinian Research Center, before flattening its structure."[133]

The Israeli siege and curfew on the Palestinian neighborhoods tightened as the army entered deeper into areas under Palestinian Authority control. Along with the standard work of destruction (in the Gaza Strip, Israeli tanks and bulldozers carried out massive housing demolition), the target of the military operations this time was Arafat's mainstream organiza-

Tanya Reinhart

tions—Fatah and the Palestinian police. As Charles Reeves described it in the *Independent:* "Mr. Sharon is bludgeoning the rickety structure of the Palestinian Authority, liquidating its police and attacking the middle-ground pro-Arafat leadership."[134] In the village of Salfit, near Nablus, an undercover Israeli death squad literally executed local Palestinian policemen. Reeves also reported eyewitnesses saying that two of the policemen, who were used to cooperating with the Israeli forces, did not hesitate to hand in their weapons to the Israeli soldiers and lie on the ground as ordered. The soldiers then executed them with a machine gun.

The center of the attacks was Arafat himself. "Arafat is no longer relevant," Sharon declared after the December 3, 2001, cabinet meeting. Shortly after that meeting, Israeli tanks surrounded Arafat's headquarters, where they imprisoned him for five months. During this period Israeli officials openly discussed the options of his exile, or even assassination. Although it was obvious that there wasn't much Arafat could do about terror when Israel's brutality was daily generating new, desperate human bombs and he himself was under siege and his police forces paralyzed, Israel and the U.S.—accompanied for a while by the European Union—nevertheless kept urging him to "act."

But no "act" of Arafat could satisfy the Israeli army. Speaking in Arabic in a televised speech on December 16, 2001, Arafat called for an end to attacks against Israelis, and stated that he had always denounced suicide bombings. Over the following days, Arafat's security forces clashed with Hamas as they carried out a wave of arrests. However, the Israeli army's chief-of-staff, Shaul Mofaz, "dismissed Arafat's crackdown on militants, saying the Palestinian Authority itself is 'infected by terror from head to toe and does everything to disrupt our lives, and to bring terrorism to our doorsteps.'"[135]

During all this, the Israeli media was celebrating. For a glimpse of the general spirit, we may look at how Yoel Marcus, a mainstream *Ha'aretz* commentator, described it:

> For the first time in a very long and controversial career, Ariel Sharon is gulping mountain air. "Sharon is holding the winning ticket," enthused *Ma'ariv*. "The Americans are behind him all the way. It's his greatest success since taking office." "The prime minister gets an A+ from the Bush administration," wrote *Yediot Aharonot*. For the first time, the European Union has criticized its darling Arafat. The UN envoy has warned Arafat that "if he doesn't change his tack, he's finished".... Rumor has it that General Zinni has described Arafat as the biggest liar he's ever met. And an American source has said what Sharon has been saying for years, namely, that "Arafat has lost his relevance as a peace partner".... Arafat has pissed off everyone, especially Bush.... Now that Arafat has descended to the low point of his days in exile in Lebanon and Tunis, and is being scolded by the

whole enlightened world, no wonder Sharon is in seventh heaven.[136]

In Western political discourse—just as in the text of the Israeli cabinet's decision of December 3, 2001—the systematic destruction of the Palestinian Authority and Arafat's rule—was described as "retaliatory acts" that always answered the last terror attack on Israeli civilians. In reality, this destruction was carefully planned long before.

THE MILITARY PLANS

By the outset of the Palestinian uprising in October 2000, Israeli military circles were ready with detailed operational plans to "topple Arafat and the Palestinian Authority." (These plans were in place well before the Palestinian uprising turned to terror. As mentioned earlier, the first terror attack on Israeli civilians during the present uprising took place on November 2, 2000.) A document prepared by Israeli General Security Service at the request of then Prime Minister Barak stated on October 15, 2000, that "Arafat, the person, is a severe threat to the security of the state [of Israel] and the damage which will result from his disappearance is less than the damage caused by his existence."[137]

The military operations are based on what is known as the "Field of Thorns" plan. In December 2000 analyst

Shraga Eilam published detailed research of the various stages of the plan, based on official sources:

> From the start of the Oslo accords, the IDF planned for the possibility that it will reoccupy the territories that had already been given to the PA. The "Field of Thorns" was developed and tested through simulations and rehearsals in 1996. During the negotiations in Camp David in July 2000, the IDF changed its training plans from a policing security operation to a full-scale military mission in which all units receive special combat anti-riot training. The code name of this operation was "Magic Tune," which prepared for a low-intensity conflict scenario. The preparations for the worst case scenario were code named "Distant World." This foresees the forceful capture of Palestinian territory by Israeli forces and the creation of a military administration, should the situation warrant such a move.[138]

The Field of Thorns plan included everything that Israel had already been executing in the first year of its oppression of the Palestinian uprising, such as "selective destruction of high-value Palestinian facilities," and "use of Israeli control of water, power, communications, and road access to limit the size and endurance of Palestinian action." Subsequent steps included "arrest [of] Palestinian Authority officials and imposition of a new military administration," and forced evacuations of Palestinian from "sensitive areas."[139]

Along with the military plans, the political plans aimed at discrediting Arafat and the Palestinian Authority were also ready right from the start. Barak's political circles worked on preparing public opinion for the eventual toppling of Arafat. On November 20, 2000, Nahman Shai, then public affairs coordinator of the Barak government, released to the press a sixty-page document titled "Palestinian Authority Non-compliance...A Record of Bad Faith and Misconduct." The document, informally referred to as the "White Book," was prepared by Barak's aide Danny Yatom.[140] The manuscript contained many of the basic themes endlessly repeated since in Israeli propaganda. Arafat was accused of "the use of an illegally armed militia—answerable to Arafat—in a low-intensity conflict masked as 'popular protest' or an 'Intifada.'" The document further claimed that at the core of Arafat's strategy was the plot to "internationalize" the conflict and "call upon the international community to replace the current structure of the process (the U.S., according to Arafat, having failed to impose 'International Legitimacy' in its Arab interpretation) with a mechanism of coercion." (Section 4.)

The White Book also accused Arafat of being the direct cause of the Palestinians' suffering (to whom the text refers as "the governed"): "Instead of responsibility for the welfare of the governed, we see him willing to use Palestinian suffering, including the death of children on the frontline, shamefully exploited." (Executive Summary.) The document goes on to illustrate Arafat's "disregard for the welfare of the governed," which "has now risen to a new level." "Thus, it [the Palestinian Authority] has systematically exploited the tragic death of the child Muhammad al-Durra at Netzarim junction—where he was caught in the crossfire of a gun battle. The P.A. was deliberately misrepresenting his death as a 'cold-blooded execution,' often several times an hour, throughout its television broadcasts." (Section 4.)

But according to the White Book these crimes of Arafat were only the most recent in a long chain of evidence that prove he never deserted the "option of violence and struggle." "As early as Arafat's own speech on the White House lawn, on September 13, 1993, there were indications that for him, the D.O.P. [Declaration of Principles] did not necessarily signify an end to the conflict. He did not, at any point, relinquish his uniform, symbolic of his status as a revolutionary commander." (Section 2.) This uniform, incidentally, is the only "indication" that the report cited of Arafat's hidden intentions on that occasion.

A large section of the document was devoted to establishing Arafat's "ambivalence and compliance" toward terrorism. "In March 1997 there was once again more than a hint of a 'green light' from Arafat to Hamas, prior to the bombing in Tel Aviv.... This is implicit in the statement made by a Hamas-affiliated member of Arafat's Cabinet, Imad Faluji, to an American paper (*Miami Herald*, April 5, 1997)." While no further hints were provided regarding how

Arafat might be implicated in the Tel Aviv bombing, this "green light to terror" theme was one that the Israeli Military Intelligence (Am'an) had been promoting since 1997 when, as we shall see, it consolidated its anti-Oslo line. Since then, this theme has been repeated again and again by military circles, and has become the mantra of Israeli propaganda: Arafat is still a terrorist and is personally responsible for the acts of all groups, from Hamas and the Islamic Jihad to Hizbollah.

By March 2001, shortly after Sharon was elected prime minister, the goal of toppling Arafat was being openly discussed. "The leading school of thought in the General Staff regarding the PA Chairman is that he is 'neither an asset, nor an [appropriate] address' for Israeli policy and action. Advocates of this line of thought, including Chief-of-Staff Shaul Mofaz and Deputy Chief-of-Staff Moshe Ya'alon, are not alarmed by the prospect of the collapse of Arafat's PA regime."[141]

Israeli media disclosed that the army's daily activities in the occupied territories were steps in a larger plan of reoccupation of these areas. On March 9, 2001, the ultimate goals of the military, authorized by Sharon, were fully spelled out in several papers. They included full "takeover" of the territories, and the re-establishment of Israeli military rule (as outlined in the advanced stages of the Field of Thorns plan). Alex Fishman, senior security correspondent for *Yediot Aharonot* explained that since Oslo, "the IDF [Israeli army] regarded the occupied territories as if they

were one territorial cell," and that "this placed some con-
straints on the IDF and enabled a certain amount of freedom for the PA and the Palestinian population." Israel's
new plan was a return to the concept of the military administration during the pre-Oslo years: The occupied territories
would be divided into tens of isolated "territorial cells,"
each of which would be assigned a special military force,
"and the local commander will have freedom to use his discretion" regarding when and whom to shoot. The IDF has
already completed the division of Gaza into territorial cells,
"but so far there has only been isolation, and not yet treatment inside the cells."[142]

Jane's Foreign Report of July 12, 2001, disclosed that
under Sharon's government, the Israeli army has updated its
plan for an "all-out assault to smash the Palestinian
Authority, force out leader Yasser Arafat and kill or detain
its army." The blueprint, titled "The Destruction of the
Palestinian Authority and Disarmament of All Armed
Forces," was presented to the Israeli government by Chief-
of-Staff Shaul Mofaz on July 8, 2001. The plan called for an
assault to be launched after a large bombing takes place in
Israel, and called for citing the bloodshed and defense
against terrorism as justification.

On November 23, 2001, Israel assassinated Hamas military leader Mahmud Abu Hanoud. Many in Israel suspect
that this assassination—just when Hamas was in its second
month of respecting an agreement with Arafat not to attack
inside Israel—was designed to provoke the appropriate

"bloodshed justification" for a counterattack on the eve of Sharon's visit to meet President George W. Bush in the United States. Even Alex Fishman of *Yediot Aharonot*, usually an obedient messenger of military sources, allowed himself a rare outburst:

Whoever gave a green light to this act of liquidation knew very well that he was thereby shattering in one blow the gentleman's agreement between Hamas and the Palestinian Authority; under that agreement, Hamas was to avoid in the then-near future inside the Green Line [Israel's border before the 1967 war], suicide bombings of the kind perpetrated at the Dolphinarium [the Tel Aviv discotheque]. Such an agreement did exist, even if neither the Palestinian Authority nor Hamas would admit it in public. It is a fact that, while the Security Service did accumulate repeated warnings of planned Hamas terrorist attacks within the Green Line, these did not materialize.... This understanding was, however, shattered by the assassination the day before yesterday—and whoever decided upon the liquidation of Abu Hanoud knew in advance that would be the price. The subject was extensively discussed both by Israel's military echelon and its political one, before it was decided to carry out the liquidation.[143]

Indeed, Hamas' bloody revenge followed a week later, just as Sharon was visiting the United States, where, as we shall see, he got his green light for the December offensive on Arafat and the Palestinian Authority.

This was but one of many instances where Israel's assassinations provoked a bloodbath of terrorist retaliation. As *Ha'aretz* analyst Uzi Benziman noted, there seems to be "a pattern of Israeli behavior that has recurred since Sharon began running the country: When a period of calm prevails in the confrontation with the Palestinians, circumstances are created that induce Israel to carry out military operations in a manner that renews, or accelerates, the cycle of violence. Previous examples: last July when Israel assassinated three Islamic Jihad men in Jenin; a month later, when Abu Ali Mustafa was assassinated in Ramallah; the liquidation of Ataf Abiat; and the killing...of Mahmoud Abu Hanoud."[144]

Following Arafat's televised speech on December 16, 2001, the truce he called for was largely respected. But on January 14, 2002, Israel assassinated Raed Karmi, the Tul Karem leader of the Al Aqsa Brigades (a group related to Arafat's Fatah movement). A lethal terror strike on a banquet hall in Hadera followed three days later, and Israel launched a new cycle of "retaliation."

Ha'aretz analyst Akiva Eldar reported that "according to a well-placed military source, just before Raed Karmi...was killed, Yasser Arafat was closer than ever to a decision to order the armed intifada to switch to nonviolent civil disobedience. The terrorist attacks and the shootings that followed Karmi's...assassination, postponed the change—but didn't cancel it. At the Palestinian Authority offices in Ramallah, officials are studying the way South African blacks challenged apartheid. Arafat has lately been speaking of a march on Jerusalem. The flood of articles written by Palestinian leaders for the Israeli and American press are [sic] an indication of the desire to turn the swords into plowshares."[145]

But the Palestinians were never given a chance to transform their struggle to civil disobedience. The military sect which rules in Israel was determined to execute its plan for undoing the Oslo arrangements and destroying Palestinian society. The bloodshed justification provided by terrorism was vital for this plan to succeed.

Anyone who witnessed the horror and pain inflicted on Israeli civilians by Palestinian terrorism would find this hard to digest. It is not just Palestinian life that does not count in Israel; those in the military sect have no reservations about sacrificing their own people. As analyst Ran Hacohen said, "In the [Israeli] junta's eyes, there are [two] kinds of human beings. First Palestinians, whose life is a nuisance one should get rid of. Second Israelis, whose life is a national asset one can liquidate when necessary. Occupation can be served by sacrificing civilians in terrorist attacks and using their death to launch a war."[146]

Israel's move to destroy the Palestinian Authority was a calculated plan, long in the making. But full execution requires first weakening the resistance of the Palestinians—

which Israel had been doing systematically since October 2000—through killings, economic strangulation, bombardment of infrastructure, imprisonment of people in their hometowns, and edging the population to the brink of starvation. Next it required international conditions to ripen for the more "advanced" steps of the plan. By December 2001, the conditions had ripened. Since then—in the new political climate defined by the September 11 attacks and the U.S.-led "war on terrorism"—anything goes.

THE U.S. ROLE

As the U.S. was preparing for its offensive in Afghanistan, many believed that the Bush administration would exert pressure on Sharon and promote some kind of "peace initiative" in order to enable the support of an Arab coalition. The script was ready from the days of the Gulf War, when, to reward the Arab world for its cooperation, the U.S. organized the Madrid conference that marked the era of an eternal "peace process." Though this allowed Israel to continue the occupation undisturbed, the apparent process of negotiations was sufficient then for the internal needs of the Arab regimes. It first appeared that the U.S. was planning a similar show at the beginning of October 2001. "The idea of a Palestinian state has always been part of a vision," Bush declared solemnly on the second of October. It was leaked that the U.S. had already prepared a detailed plan for a peace settlement, which was only frozen because of the September

11 events. We heard that a draft of a speech by Secretary of State Colin Powell was prepared for the event, which he was soon to find the right occasion to deliver.

Few in the Western media expressed the kind of skepticism that this leak was met with in the Arab media. As Michael Jansen noted in *Jordanian Time:* "The timing of the Bush remark and the leak are important. They came on the eve of visits by U.S. Defense Secretary Donald Rumsfeld to Egypt, Saudi Arabia and Oman. Washington is eager to convince these governments to permit the use of their territory for the coming offensive against Afghanistan.... Once again, Arab governments are supposed to sign on to a US program of action without any concrete quid pro quo.... Thus, a vague Bush statement and a leak by an anonymous official of the existence of a plan which is not revealed are supposed to convince the Arabs that the administration has good intentions."[147]

The "peace initiatives" intensified around the October 9, 2001, emergency meeting of the Organization of Islamic Conference (OIC), a body including fifty-six countries whose silence or cooperation was extremely important to the United States at that moment. During this stage, more details were leaked to make it all look concrete, and a Bush spokesman, British Prime Minister Tony Blair, entered the picture. Blair, who had returned to London from a two-day visit to the United Arab Emirates, Oman, and Egypt, was quite open in explaining the urgency: "One thing becoming increasingly clear to me is the need to upgrade our media and public opinion operations in the Arab and Muslim world."[148] This PR phase culminated when Blair and Arafat staged a joint press conference on October 15, 2001.

However, on October 18, 2001, Aluf Benn reported in *Ha'aretz* that "according to a U.S. report," Powell was leaning toward canceling his plans to deliver a speech on United States policy in the Middle East. "According to the report, policy makers in the American administration feel that there is no longer a need for a Powell speech because President George Bush has already presented his vision for the Middle East in statements over the past few weeks. With the cancellation of Powell's speech, most of the steps planned by the administration for increased involvement in the Middle East will have been removed from the agenda...American diplomats sent a message to Sharon this week saying that the administration has no plans to launch a Middle East diplomatic initiative in the near future, and that any steps will be coordinated with Israel in advance."[149]

If the U.S. ever wanted to halt Israel even temporarily, it could do so easily and at any moment by immediately freezing all military aid. Instead, on October 24, 2001, the day the headlines announced that Bush's and Powell's patience with Israel was giving out, the U.S. Senate approved $2.76 billion in assistance for Israel, more money than it gives any other country in the world. Out of this sum, $2.04 billion was earmarked for special military aid.

It became even clearer that the U.S. gave full backing to Israel's aggression after America began its offensive in

Afghanistan. During his trip to Washington in December, Sharon got a green light for the massive December operation against the Palestinian Authority and the siege against Arafat. As I wrote at the time:

> If at first it seemed that the U.S. will try to keep the Arab world on its side by some tokens of persuasion, as it did during the Gulf War, it is now clear that they couldn't care less. U.S. policy is no longer based on building coalitions or investing in persuasion, but on sheer force. The smashing 'victory' in Afghanistan has sent a clear message to the Third-World that nothing can stop the U.S. from targeting any nation for destruction. They seem to believe that the most sophisticated weapons of the twenty-first century...can sustain them as the sole rulers of the world forever. From now on, fear should be the sufficient condition for obedience. The U.S. hawks, who are pushing to expand the war to Iraq view Israel as an asset. As Prof. Alain Joxe, head of the French CIRPES (Peace and Strategic Studies) has put it in *Le Monde*, "the American leadership is presently shaped by dangerous right wing...extremists, who seek to use Israel as an offensive tool to destabilize the whole Middle East area" (December 17, 2001).[150]

Three months later, the Bush administration allowed Sharon to order Israel's most massive offensive against the

West Bank towns and villages—Operation Defensive Shield. As always, this was preceded by an apparently energetic "peace initiative" launched by the U.S. in March 2002. United States special envoy Anthony Zinni was sent to the area with the declared goal of achieving a cease-fire based on the plan proposed by CIA head George Tenet in June 2001. Zinni's tour was reinforced by a visit from Vice President Dick Cheney on March 19, 2002. Israel quickly declared that it welcomed the cease-fire idea and agreed to the immediate implementation of the Tenet plan. Although the Palestinian Authority produced identical declarations and called on opposition organizations to show restraint, Israel eventually declared that the cease-fire negotiations based on the Tenet plan failed because of the Palestinians' usual rejectionism.

What received no attention whatsoever was the fact that Israel never actually agreed to implement the Tenet plan. That plan contained the requirement that the Israeli military forces must withdraw to the positions they held before September 28, 2000 (when Israel began ordering its forces into areas under the control of the Palestinian Authority, following Sharon's provocation at Temple Mount). As was openly disclosed in the Israeli media, the Israeli side did not accept this central demand—all it had been willing to offer was to ease the siege in areas where the Palestinians manifested good behavior.[151] There was not even a hint on the U.S. side that it demanded real Israeli adherence to the Tenet plan. On the contrary, Israel's "good will" was highly praised.

Throughout the "cease-fire" negotiations, Israel continued its siege on Arafat's headquarters and its daily "operations" against the Palestinian Authority in Ramallah and several refugee camps, clearly providing no opportunity for the Palestinian Authority to act to restrain terror attacks. It was obvious that the next terror attack was inevitable. While the U.S. enabled all that, the *Washington Post* disclosed on March 24, 2002, that "Israeli newspapers have also reported in recent days that Sharon has told the Bush administration to expect an escalation if no cease-fire is achieved. For instance, Shimon Schiffer, arguably Israel's best-connected political reporter, wrote in the newspaper *Yediot Aharonot* today that when Vice President Cheney visited Israel last week, Sharon 'reached an agreement' with him that if Zinni's mission fails, Washington would support Israeli strikes on the Palestinians. U.S. officials did not deny the report."[152]

CHAPTER VIII

APRIL-JUNE 2002
THE RETURN OF MILITARY
OCCUPATION

OPERATION DEFENSIVE SHIELD

On March 29, 2002, following a murderous terror attack on the eve of Jewish Passover, Israel launched its long-awaited and carefully planned offensive on Palestinian cities and refugee camps in the West Bank that completely destroyed all institutions of the Palestinian Authority, and left the West Bank in ruins. At the outset of the invasion, the Israeli army penetrated Arafat's compound in Ramallah, confining the imprisoned Arafat and the small group with him to just one small wing of the compound, with all electricity cut and communication reduced to cell phones. (Arafat's trapped group was later joined by members of the International Solidarity Movement who managed to enter the wing.) A succinct summary of the destruction of the Palestinian infrastructure during that military operation is provided by Mouin Rabbani, director of the Palestinian-American Research Center in Ramallah:

Operation Defensive Shield was quantitatively as well as qualitatively different from anything which had preceded it. The army's attempt to eliminate paramilitary organizations such as the Fatah-affiliated al Aqsa Martyrs' Brigades, the Izz al Din al Qassam Brigades of Hamas and others which have spearheaded the armed uprising formed only part of a much broader campaign...Palestinian security facilities were systematically destroyed in every Palestinian town and village occupied, and security personnel were disarmed and detained en masse. PA ministries and civil agencies were ransacked, vandalized and sometimes looted as well. Private property, public facilities, commercial establishments, nongovernmental organizations and offices maintained by the various Palestinian political factions sustained extensive damage, and were in many cases looted or destroyed altogether. Such actions typically occurred not in the course of armed conflict, but well after the military established control.[153]

But the destruction of Palestinian institutions pales compared to the suffering, casualties, and injuries inflicted on the Palestinian people during the course of the "operation." It will be some time before the stream of tormented witnesses and cries for help that poured in from all over the besieged Palestinian communities during the dark month of

April 2002 are documented in full. Let us continue to confine ourselves here to Rabbani's factual summary.

As confirmed by Israeli soldiers in newspaper reports, Palestinian noncombatants were pressed into service as human shields, forced to knock on doors, open suspicious packages and were even deployed in combat operations. Residents of occupied towns and villages were placed under strict, round-the-clock curfew for the duration of the Israeli military presence, with virtually no exceptions made for urgent humanitarian cases whether resulting from conflict-related injuries or otherwise. Those venturing outdoors (including women, children and the elderly) risked being shot without warning by snipers.... In Nablus and Jenin, the curfew was maintained for almost the entire duration of the occupation, with water and electricity to most residents severed. Israeli forces prevented both Palestinian and international medical and rescue services from operation through the threat and use of violence, leading to an unknown number of deaths from otherwise treatable wounds and regular medical conditions. Troops also invaded hospitals and clinics, in several cases arresting patients from their beds and ransacking the premises. Thousands of males aged 15–45 were detained in tents without food, water, toilet facilities or blankets. Many reported torture and abuse in detention. Most were eventually released, but some 1,500 have been incarcerated without charge or trial for an initial six-month period or pending formal charges.[154]

Israel committed daily war crimes during that invasion, but the pit of the horror was in Jenin. The Jenin refugee camp and the Casbah in Nablus were considered by the Israeli army to be the toughest areas to conquer. Preparations to seize these areas began long in advance. In January 2002, Amir Oren reported in *Ha'aretz* that the army was studying historical precedents, including the German takeover of the Warsaw Ghetto: "In order to prepare properly for the next campaign, one of the Israeli officers in the territories said...[that] it's justified—and in fact essential—to learn from every possible source. If the mission will be to seize a densely populated refugee camp, or take over the Casbah in Nablus, and if the commander's obligation is to try to execute the mission without casualties on either side, then he must first analyze and internalize the lessons of earlier battles—even, however shocking it may sound, even how the German army fought in the Warsaw ghetto."[155]

Nablus and Jenin were the only places where the Palestinians showed a real, stubborn resistance to Israel's invading army. In Nablus, the Israeli army used the same methods as in Jenin—heavy shelling and bulldozing that sowed destruction in the old Casbah and killed seventy-five people, many of whom were civilians. But then the army decided not to risk combing through the town's narrow alleyways and engaging in full house-to-house combat. In the case of Jenin, the army's advance decision was to go all the way in and break the back of the resistance at the center of the refugee camp.[156] "A senior commander said that 'we are even considering bringing F16 planes…. He explained that the main reservation is 'the security range,' namely the fear that IDF soldiers will be hurt in the bombardment."[157] On April 9, 2002—the seventh day of fierce fighting in Jenin—thirteen Israeli soldiers were killed in battle. The military reaction was a decision to erase the entire center of the camp even though many of the residents were still hiding in their homes.

JENIN—THE UNTOLD CRIME

What is particularly frightening about the events of Jenin is how Israel managed to cover up its crimes, and silence protesting voices. Although ample information and images made it to the international media, the final conclusion was that we can't really know what happened there. As Irit Katriel wrote: "Only an unbelievably brutal world can look at the remains of what was once home for 13,000 impoverished 1948 Palestinian refugees, scratch its head and say 'we don't know what actually happened in the Jenin refugee camp.' The camp is now described by the media as an 'earthquake zone,' a natural disaster of sorts. Unlike real earthquake zones, you don't see massive search and rescue teams in this one.... Only the survivors and a handful of Red Crescent workers are there to search the rubble for the corpses, guided by their stench. Man-made earthquakes do not, apparently, warrant real relief efforts."[158]

On the sixth day of the "operation" in Jenin, just before the thirteen soldiers were killed, Israeli security and political echelons became alarmed by the invasion's disastrous effects. "Officers of the IDF expressed their shock" about what was happening there: "Because of the risks, the bulldozers simply 'shave' the houses, leading to enormous destruction. When the world sees the pictures of what we have done there, it will cause us enormous damage."[159] Israeli Foreign Minister Shimon Peres even slipped and mentioned the taboo word "massacre" (which he immediately denied, of course). That was before the real "erasing" of the camp started, the following day.

In Israel, these alarming revelations about Jenin were perceived as a public relations crisis, and a propaganda battle was immediately launched. "The Foreign Ministry is mobilizing forces to counter Palestinian allegations that IDF forces conducted 'a massacre' in the Jenin refugee camp."[160] The IDF and Foreign Ministry set up a special PR center in Jerusalem, and its representative, Gideon Meir, passed on to the press the major principles of the Israeli version of events: (a) "What happened in Jenin was a fierce battle and not a massacre" and (b) "The battle was fierce because the IDF sought to minimize civilian suffering."[161]

These messages have since been repeated again and again,

not only by politicians and Israeli government and military spokespeople, but also by reporters, analysts, and columnists—they are woven into news reports, or disguised as spontaneous acts of expressing an educated opinion. Here is *Ha'aretz*'s editorial version of the propaganda line: "There is evidence of intense combat, but, with appropriate caution, it can already be said what did not happen in the Jenin refugee camp. There was no massacre. No order from above was given, nor was a local initiative executed, to deliberately and systematically kill unarmed people."[162]

This line is quite sophisticated. The word "massacre" may bring to mind soldiers moving from house to house, shooting everyone they find—men, women, and children (as occurred in Sabra and Shatila in Lebanon). Such a form of massacre clearly did not take place in Jenin. No Palestinian source ever described the facts that way. Still, *Ha'aretz* and everyone else insist on falsifying only this specific interpretation of the word "massacre." What did clearly happen in Jenin was that the Israeli forces simply ignored the fact that there were an unknown number of civilians in the areas that they attacked day and night with missiles from Cobra helicopters and demolished with bulldozers, in order to clear the way for the invading tanks. No one came to execute these people individually; they were crushed and buried under their bombed or bulldozed homes. Others died of their wounds in alleys, or cried for days under the ruins, until their voices faded away.

Bit by bit, testimony from reserve soldiers began filtering

into the back pages of the Israeli media: "After the first moments of the fighting, when a commander was killed...the instructions were clear: shoot every window, spray every house—whether someone shoots from there or not." To the question of whether he saw civilians get hurt, the reservist answered: "Personally, no. But the point is that they were inside the houses. The last days, the majority of those who came out of the houses were old people, women and children, who were there the whole time and absorbed our fire. These people were not given any chance to leave the camp, and we are talking about many people."[163]

Ordinary language allows the use of the word "massacre" for such cases of indiscriminate killing of civilians. But the issue is not language. The eyewitness account of the reserve soldier, and the others we will turn to, is sufficient to make most people shiver, whether or not they would call it a massacre. For the success of the PR campaign, it was therefore necessary to stress that what happened in Jenin was not a blind shelling and killing of civilians, but a fierce battle in which civilians may have also occasionally gotten killed. The PR center clarified this in that second message quoted above.

In the Jenin refugee camp, where 15,000 residents were densely crowded, there were dozens, perhaps even hundreds, of armed Palestinian fighters, some of whom were wanted terrorists. They were determined to show resistance and booby-trapped the roads and alleys of the camp. What is considered appropriate for such battle conditions? By the logic of Israeli propaganda, it was possible to erase the whole camp, along with its residents, with a few precise hits from some F-16 bomber jets, and thus eliminate all the terrorists and fighters with zero casualties to the Israeli army. Instead, the army took enormous risks and sustained losses by actually fighting on the ground, a measure, it argued, taken in order to save Palestinian lives. If we accept this as the only range of options, the Israeli army proved in Jenin that it is a truly humane army.

Alarmed by the stream of horrified witnesses, the UN Security Council voted unanimously on April 19, 2002, to send a fact-finding mission to Jenin. "The 150 vote came hours after Foreign Minister Shimon Peres told [UN Secretary-General] Annan that Israel would welcome a UN representative 'to clarify the facts' of what happened in Jenin refugee camp. 'Israel has nothing to hide regarding the operation in Jenin,' Peres told Annan. 'Our hands are clean.'"[164] Secretary General Kofi Annan proceeded to appoint a three-member fact-finding team, led by former Finnish president Martti Ahtisaari. The other members were Cornelio Sommaruga, former president of the International Committee of the Red Cross, and Sadako Ogata, the former UN High Commissioner for Refugees who is Japan's special envoy on Afghan reconstruction. Annan also appointed as military adviser retired U.S. general William Nash, who was the UN administrator in the divided Kosovo city of Mitrovica, and a police adviser, Peter Fitzgerald of Ireland, the former head of the UN international police force in Bosnia.

But this highly respectable team was immediately

attacked by Israel. At first, "government sources said the makeup of the commission was 'the lesser of evils' but expressed a fear that the backgrounds of Ogata and Sommaruga in humanitarian affairs could backfire on Israel."[165] The next day, government sources said that the committee's makeup was "very bad for Israel, since it is political-diplomatic in character, not military-professional as necessitated by the situation...Israel is particularly opposed to the inclusion of the former president of the International Red Cross, Cornelio Sommaruga. The sources said Israel has evidence of anti-Semitic statements made by Sommaruga in the past."[166] Sharon announced that Israel was not going to cooperate with the team, a position it maintained despite Annan's attempts at some compromise. The U.S. backed Israel, first silently and later explicitly. On May 1, 2002, the Security Council decided to disband the fact-finding committee, and under the threat of a U.S. veto, proposals to pursue the investigation in other ways were dropped.[167]

Sharon hurried to publicly thank the U.S. for its help on the matter: "Likening Israel's fight in the Mideast to the U.S. campaign against al Qaeda terrorists, Israeli Prime Minister Ariel Sharon...credited the Bush administration with helping scuttle plans for a U.N. inquiry into the Israeli attack on the Jenin refugee camp...'We could have been trapped in a very complicated situation,' Sharon said in an evening speech to the Anti-Defamation League, a Jewish organization...Sharon said President Bush, Secretary of State

Colin Powell and other U.S. officials had been influential in helping get the fact-finding mission disbanded."[168]

Since there was no formal investigation, the story of Jenin remains untold, and Israel's official version that nothing even remotely resembling a massacre took place in Jenin became acceptable. Thus, Israel won the propaganda battle. Still, this does not mean we know nothing of what happened there. Let us just look at some of the crimes that should be investigated in the future, and pursued through international courts.

Certainly, soldiers did not move from house to house systematically shooting everybody they found—men, women, and children. But they did execute unarmed men. Here is a fragment of one testimony, reported by the *Independent*:

> Fathi Shalabi watched his son die. The two men were standing side by side with their hands up when Israeli soldiers opened fire on them. Mr. Shalabi's son, Wadh, and another man who was with them died instantly, but the 63-year-old Mr. Shalabi survived. He lay on the ground pretending to be dead for more than an hour while his son's blood gathered around him…. Mr. Shalabi described what took place. Soldiers ordered his family and Mr. Al Sadi down a narrow alley. "In cover behind the corner were four soldiers. The two young men with me were carrying baby children, and the soldiers did not shoot at them." Wadh Shalabi was carrying his four-month-old son, Mahmoud. The sol-

diers ordered the men to hand the children over to their mothers and told the women and children to go into the next door house. Then they ordered the men to raise their shirts and show they were not wearing suicide belts. "The soldiers were about three meters away. I heard the names of two of them; they were Gaby and David." He said that the soldier called Gaby appeared to be in command. "They saw Abdul Karim had a plaster[169] on his back. Suddenly Gaby shouted 'Kill them!'"[170]

The two men who were murdered were civilians. However, even shooting surrendering soldiers is a war crime. The Hague Tribunal found Bosnian Serb general Radislav Krstic guilty of genocide for his role in the killing of Muslim soldiers and males in Srebrenica in 1995. (Muslim women and children were not killed, but expelled from the town. In Kosovo's mass graves as well, mostly male bodies were found.)

One of the most demonic innovations of Operation Defensive Shield was the use of giant Caterpillar D-9 bull-dozers manufactured for civilian use as military weapons. Here is how Rory MacMillan of *The Scotsman* described his first encounter with these metal monsters in Beit Lehem: "On Saturday, for the first time since I arrived here, I could not believe my eyes. Much of what you see in a war zone is, as you would expect, not so different from the television pictures.... A town under foreign occupation after invasion is as smashed up as you would imagine. What I saw yesterday, however, is beyond imagination: Israeli bulldozers the size of houses. At the back of them, enormous claws were poised for ripping up streets and buildings to make way for tanks and to destroy the homes of suicide bombers."[171]

There are testimonies that in Jenin, as the D-9s were erasing the center of the refugee camp, an unknown number of people were bulldozed alive inside their homes. This did not happen only in Jenin. The bulldozers were first used in Nablus—the heart of Palestinian resistance—which the Israeli army had not yet risked conquering. According to testimonies collected and researched by B'tselem, an Israeli human rights group, on April 6, 2002, the huge bulldozers demolished houses in the Al Quarim neighborhood. The A-Sha'abi family were trapped inside their house, whose exits were blocked by the debris remaining from the neighboring houses demolished earlier. The A-Sha'abis shouted and signaled to the bulldozer driver, but to no avail. Nine members of the family died under the rubble. Their bodies were recovered six days later, when the army left, together with the survivors, Abdalla A-Sha'abi and his wife, who gave the testimony.[172]

But in Jenin, the use of bulldozers became maniacal. In an extended reportage, *Yediot Aharonot* disclosed that the order to send them to wipe out the whole center of the camp was made on April 9, 2002, following the loss of the thirteen Israeli soldiers. "The decision to go full force with the D-niners was perhaps expected for those who participated in the traumatic battle in Jenin. What was less expected was the extent of the operation: Full erasure of the houses in the 'hundred by hundred' [the unofficial name used by the soldiers for the center of the camp, the size of a soccer field]. In practice, no one told the D-niners in advance that was the goal. They understood it as the commands started pouring into the cockpits. The dozen destruction instruments were divided among the four units that circled the area...and started systematic destruction."[173]

Tsadok Yehezkeli of *Yediot Aharonot* has worked relentlessly to expose the facts about the bulldozer unit and its operation in Jenin, including a chilling interview with one of the operators. The text speaks for itself.

> The speaker is Moshe Nissim.... In the Jenin refugee camp, he was called over the military radio: Kurdi Bear. Kurdi [Curd], because this is the name he insisted on. Bear, after the D9 he was driving, demolishing house after house.... Kurdi Bear was considered the most devoted, brave and probably the most destructive operator.... A man that the Jenin camp inquiry committee would want very much to have a word with. For 75 hours, with no break, he sat on the huge bulldozer, charges exploding around him, and erased house after house. His story, which he tells openly and with no inhibitions, is far from being a regular war myth:
>
> ...I entered Jenin driven by madness, by despera-

tion, I felt I have nothing to lose, that even if I "get it," no big deal. I told my wife: If anything happens to me, at least someone will take care of you! I started my reserve service in the worst conditions possible. Maybe this is why I didn't give a damn.... My life was in deep shit for the past one and a half years. For almost half a year I am suspended from work as a senior inspector in the Jerusalem municipality....

During my obligatory regular service [years before] I was constantly sentenced to prison, because I refused to be a vehicle electrician. In my [reserves] unit as well, in the tractor unit, I was supposed to be an electrician, but actually, I did nothing, just messed around.... Truth is, they didn't even know me. When I am given responsibility, I can act differently.... This time was one of those moments. What haven't I done for them to take me? I sent the guys to twist the battalion commander's arm.... I pleaded with the battalion commander. Finally, he agreed to give me a chance.

The funny bit is, I didn't even know how to operate the D9. I have never been an operator. But I begged them to give me a chance to learn. Before we went into Sh'khem [Nablus], I asked some of the guys to teach me. They sat with me for two hours. They taught me how to drive forwards and make a flat surface....

When we got into the [Jenin] camp, the D9's were already waiting. They were hauled from Sh'khem [Nablus]. I got the big D9 L, me and the Yemenite, my partner.... The moment I drove the tractor into the camp, something switched in my head. I went mad. All the desperation, caused by my personal condition, just vanished at once. All that remained was the anger over what had happened to our guys [the soldiers]....

Everything was booby-trapped. Even the walls of houses. Just touch them, and they blow up. Or, they would shoot you the moment you entered. There were charges in the roads, under the floor, between the walls.... For me, in the D9, it was nothing...Even 80 Kilos of explosives only rattled the tractor's blade.... It's a monster. A tank can get hit in the belly. Its belly is sensitive. With the D9, you should only look out for RPG's or 50 Kilos of explosives on the roof. But I didn't think about it then....

Do you know how I held out for 75 hours? I didn't get off the tractor. I had no problem of fatigue, because I drank whisky all the time. I had a bottle in the tractor at all times. I had put them in my bag in advance. Everybody else took clothes, but I knew what was waiting for me there, so I took whisky and something to munch on.... For 75 hours I didn't think about my life at home, about all the problems. Everything was erased. Sometimes images of terror attacks in Jerusalem crossed my mind. I witnessed some of them....

For three days, I just destroyed and destroyed. The whole area. Any house that they fired from came down. And to knock it down, I tore down some more. They were warned by loudspeaker to get out of the house before I come, but I gave no one a chance. I didn't wait. I didn't give one blow, and wait for them to come out. I would just ram the house with full power, to bring it down as fast as possible. I wanted to get to the other houses. To get as many as possible.... Others may have restrained themselves, or so they say. Who are they kidding?...I didn't give a damn about the Palestinians, but I didn't just ruin with no reason. It was all under orders.

Many people were inside houses we started to demolish. They would come out of the houses we were working on. I didn't see, with my own eyes, people dying under the blade of the D9. And I didn't see houses falling down on live people. But if there were any, I wouldn't care at all. I am sure people died inside these houses, but it was difficult to see, there was lots of dust everywhere, and we worked a lot at night. I found joy with every house that came down, because I knew they [the Palestinians] didn't mind dying, but they cared for their homes. If you knocked down a house, you buried 40 or 50 people for generations. If I am sorry for anything, it is for not tearing the whole camp down.[174]

The bulldozer unit was highly commended in Israel for its achievements in Jenin. On June 5, 2002, a month after the UN inquiry commission was disbanded, the unit got a medal for distinction in battle. Reserve Major Amos Ido, who commanded the bulldozer unit in Jenin told Tsadok Yehezkeli: "Till Jenin we were considered blue color workers, in the background. Since Jenin, the attitude towards us has changed.... Our place in the military practice has changed: Today, in every exercise and in every military operation—you can't even conceive of going out to the target without a bulldozer."[175]

The biggest controversy that any future investigation should tackle is the number of Palestinian victims in Jenin. The battle over the body count has been crucial in Israel's claim that there was no massacre in Jenin. To date, the official Israeli version is that only about forty-five bodies were recovered, and the total number of dead is estimated at about fifty-five.

Under the conditions of ruin in the West Bank following Operation Defensive Shield, and in the absence of a proper investigation, the Palestinians have not been able to immediately establish their estimate of the actual number of people killed by the Israeli siege. Many of the residents of the ruined Jenin camp fled to neighboring villages. As we shall see, since Operation Defensive Shield, all towns and villages of the West Bank have been completely sealed, with access almost impossible from the outside. A thorough investigation requires going over the lists of residents in the camp, tracing those who relocated to isolated places to find out who is missing, and obtaining precise lists of the detainees whom Israel still holds. All of these requirements would be virtually impossible to carry out under the present conditions. The lists of refugee residents are in the hands of UNRWA, which has been under too much pressure lately to conduct such investigation itself. (Recall that all computerized resources of the Palestinian Authority were destroyed in the operation.) Such investigation requires enormous human resources—field workers tracing and interviewing those who escaped from the Jenin camp. Palestinian society is now struggling with the most basic questions of survival, and does not have immediate access to the resources needed to conduct such an investigation. A Human Rights Watch team that hastily agreed to the estimated number of fifty-five dead in its report of May 2, 2002, certainly could not conduct such an investigation, and restricted itself to interviewing the survivors who stayed in the Jenin camp.[176]

So, on this issue as well, Israel's version became established in public consciousness as correct. Nevertheless, even prior to a real investigation, many question marks arise in an examination of the Israeli press.

Though Jenin was sealed to the media, pictures of the battlefield, shot with local amateur video cameras, were broadcast, mainly on Arab TV. They showed alleys lined up with male bodies (many armed). This was to be expected, given that there was indeed a serious battle in Jenin. The early reports of the Israeli army estimated two hundred Palestinian bodies. The Palestinian figures were much higher. As the time approached to open the camp to the press, the army expressed, as we saw, serious concerns regarding the "PR" effects of the scenes on the ground. It is appropriate to wonder what happened to the bodies witnessed by these early reports.

On Friday, April 12, 2002, it was reported that "the IDF intends to bury today Palestinians killed in the West Bank camp. Around 200 Palestinians are believed to have been killed in clashes with Israeli soldiers since the start of the operation last week.... Military sources said that until now the IDF has not buried any of the bodies. The sources said that two infantry companies, along with members of the military rabbinate, will enter the camp today to collect the bodies. Those who can be identified as civilians will be moved to a hospital in Jenin, and then on to burial, while those identified as terrorists will be buried at a special cemetery in the Jordan Valley. One Israeli source said that the decision to bury the bodies was taken to prevent the Palestinians from using the bodies for propaganda purposes.... The Palestinian Authority has expressed concerns that Israel is trying to hide the large number of dead, since it has blocked Palestinian medical teams from evacuating the dead and wounded from the camp during the past week."[177]

Apparently, no one in Israel was particularly concerned then about issues of international law, war crimes, mass graves, etc. So the evening before, further information was provided on Israeli TV about the preparations, including showing the special refrigerated trucks that were waiting to transfer bodies to "terrorist cemeteries" in the Jordan Valley. However, a petition to the high court interfered. "The High Court of Justice issued an interim order Friday blocking the IDF from moving out the bodies of dead Palestinians from the Jenin refugee camp in the West Bank. A panel of three justices will hold a full discussion on the matter [Sunday] morning, following a petition by Adalah, the Legal Center for Arab Minority Rights in Israel and LAW, The Palestinian Society for the Protection of Human Rights.... The petitioners claim the army's decision violates international law as the Jordan Valley cemetery will, they claim, be basically a mass grave, thus damaging the honor of the dead."[178]

Right-wing PM Avigdor Lieberman (National Union Yisrael Beiteinu) was furious with the decision and called for the high court president Aharon Barak to be removed from his post following the IDF decision. "Barak's decision is a vulgar and clear interference by the judiciary in the decision of the executive..." he argued.[179] His worry may have been premature. When the full discussion was held on Sunday , the high court turned down the petitions, while recommending that "the army make use of the services of the Red Crescent and local officials in Jenin to help locate and identify bodies, subject to the considerations of the military commanders."[180]

It was reported that following the temporary High Court decision on Friday, the IDF stopped clearing the bodies from the camp, waiting for the final decision on Sunday: "In light of the court's decision, issued by Supreme Court President Aharon Barak, the IDF stopped clearing the bodies from the camp Friday. Some of the bodies had already been removed from the camp Thursday and moved to a site near Jenin, but had not been buried."[181] However, on Sunday, the media were finally allowed to the camp, and they found a scene of mass destruction—but with roads clean of bodies: That's how Amos Har'el described it in *Ha'aretz:* "The visit, which the army allowed after a critical three-day delay, did not provide an unequivocal answer to the question that everyone continues to fight over—the Israeli leaders and their spokesmen, and the Palestinians—how many Palestinians died during the fighting? We talked with soldiers in Jenin, officers and rank-and-file troopers, and all vehemently denied the accusations of a massacre of civilians. The Palestinian residents who escaped gave reporters a completely different version. But on the ground, yesterday, only one Palestinian body was to be found in the open, in an area where most of the fighting took place."[182]

Har'el asks: "So what happened to the rest of the bodies?... IDF Spokesman Brigadier General Ron Kitri said on Friday there were some 200 [bodies], but then corrected himself with a much lower figure." The formal IDF answer was given that same day: "Israel Defense Forces officers now estimate that dozens—not hundreds—of Palestinians were killed as a result of the army's activities in the Jenin refugee camp. As of last night, 46 Palestinian corpses have been located in the camp. Updated estimates concerning the total number of Palestinian fatalities in the camp now range between 70 and a little over 100. Officials believe that some of the corpses are still buried under the rubble of houses demolished by IDF bulldozers."[183]

Not too many further questions were asked in Israel regarding how the IDF's initial estimate of two hundred dead in Jenin turned out to be so overexaggerated. As time went by, official Israeli estimates of the total number of dead in Jenin went down further to fifty-five. Miraculously, after ten days of hell, the number of dead in Jenin turned out to be even lower than that in Nablus, where Israel's estimated number of dead was seventy-five. Like anything else surrounding the Jenin crime, the truth about the number of dead, and the fate of their bodies, awaits proper international investigation.

PENAL COLONIES

By the end of April 2002, the Israeli army was reaching the completion of Operation Defensive Shield's objectives. The Palestinian Authority, along with most of Palestinian society's civil institutions, was ruined. As for the goal of "toppling Arafat," at first it seemed that Arafat's popularity had only increased during his long imprisonment, when he was perceived as a symbol of Palestinian resistance. However, in the end Arafat surrendered, as he has so often before in his career, and again lost the trust of his people. On May 1, 2002, he was released from his besieged quarters within the framework of a U.S.-brokered deal. In return, he agreed to the expulsion of thirteen of his armed militiamen who were under siege in the Bethlehem Nativity Church, and to U.S-Israeli supervised "reforms" of the Palestinian Authority. While Palestinian society would welcome real reforms in the direction of democratization, Israel and the U.S. made it clear that what they meant by "reforms" was the formation of new Palestinian security forces whose collaboration with Israel can be guaranteed, under the supervision of the United States (and, possibly, also Egypt).

Sharon has repeatedly clarified that the "reforms" required of the Palestinians should follow the Afghan model. "Under Sharon's plan, security reforms in the PA would be carried out within thirty days, and a provisional state would be established within a year, as in Afghanistan, with an alternative leadership asking for a mandate in national elections. Sharon agrees to renew diplomatic negotiations following the year of reforms."[184] The mention of national elections may sound soothing, and would certainly be welcomed by Palestinian society had the elections any real content. But the analogy to Afghanistan makes their real content clear: In the Afghan model, the new "leadership" was imported from the outside by the U.S., and imposed on the Afghan people after a massive bombardment and devastation of the country.

In any case, Sharon and his military echelons kept insisting after Arafat's release that no reforms were possible as long as Arafat had any power, and that he should be completely "neutralized." On June 24, 2002, while Israel was launching a new offensive in the West Bank, Bush fully endorsed Sharon's vision in a "long awaited policy statement on the Middle East conflict." Though he did not mention Arafat by name, Bush was clearly calling for his removal. He said that peace needed "new and different Palestinian leadership.... When the Palestinians have new leaders, institutions and security arrangements, the U.S. will support the creation of a Palestinian state."[185] In Israel, this was conceived as a smashing victory for Sharon's policy. Israel's foreign minister Shimon Peres, who up to that point was announcing periodically that Arafat was still a partner (while serving in a government whose declared goal was to topple Arafat), joined in with the choir. "Peres told the opening session of the Labor Party convention that in the new reality created by U.S. President George Bush's speech last week, Israel must 'seek or create an appropriate partner for the war on terrorism, one suitable for peace.'"[186]

With the destruction of the Palestinian Authority, the road was open for the full implementation of the "reoccupation" plan. In Chapter VII we saw that while Israel presents all its military acts as spontaneous reactions to terror, the fact of the matter is that this plan had already been fully spelled out in the Israeli media back in March 2001, soon after Sharon entered office. It outlined a return to the concept of the military administration during the pre-Oslo years: The occupied territories would be divided into tens of isolated "territorial cells," each of which would be assigned a special military force.[187]

In practice, since Operation Defensive Shield in April 2002, the West Bank has already been divided into "territorial cells." The towns and villages there have been completely sealed. Even exit by foot, which was possible up to that point, became blocked, and movement between the "cells" requires formal permits from the Israeli military authorities. Soldiers and snipers prevent any "unauthorized" walking to the fields, to places of work and study, or to medical treatment. On June 19, 2002 (again, following a week of terror attacks), Israel launched another military offensive in the West Bank—Operation Determined Path—designed to complete the military takeover.

At the time, Israeli public discourse was busy with plans for a "separation" of Israel and the Palestinians, which would involve building a physical fence around the West Bank. To get a picture of what this separation model means, recall the situation in the Gaza Strip, which we examined in Chapter I. During the Oslo years, the Gaza Strip became a huge prison, surrounded with electric fences and army posts, completely sealed off from the outside world. About one-third of its land was confiscated for the six thousand Israeli settlers living there (and their defense array), while over a million Palestinians were crowded in the remaining areas of the prison. This prison has been further divided into smaller "cells" that can be isolated from each other at the will of the Israeli army. The living conditions in Gaza deteriorated even more during the Israeli oppression of the Palestinian uprising. With no work or sources of income, about 80 percent of its residents now depend for their living on the relief agency UNRWA, or contributions from Arab states and charity organizations. The population is on the verge of starvation, with malnutrition symptoms already found in children. At the outset of its June offensive, the Israeli cabinet "decided in principle in favor of the expulsion of families of suicide strikers from the West Bank to the Gaza Strip."[188] As a senior Israeli analyst stated, Gaza can now serve as "the penal colony" of Israel, its "devils island [sic], Alcatraz."[189]

This is the future that Sharon and the Israeli army have in mind for the West Bank as well. While the external fence was being built, Israel's June 2002 military operation was designed to complete the division of the internal prison cells.

However, unlike the pre-Oslo period of Israeli military rule, the army makes it clear that there is no intention to construct any civil administration that will take care of the basic daily needs of the two million Palestinians in the West Bank, needs such as food supplies, health services, and garbage and sewage facilities. For these tasks, some form of a Palestinian Authority will be maintained, though in practice it will not be allowed to function.

As a "military source" told *Ha'aretz* in June 2002, "Internal conclusions of the security echelons, following operation 'Defensive Shield,' assessed that the functioning of the civil branches of the Palestinian Authority had reached an unprecedented nadir, mainly due to the destruction the IDF operation left behind in Ramallah (including the systematic destruction of computers and databases).... Combined with the severe restrictions on movement, the Palestinian population is becoming, as the military source defined it, 'poor, dependent, unemployed, rather hungry, and extreme'.... The financial reserves of the Palestinian Authority are reaching the bottom.... In a future not far off, the majority of Palestinians will only be able to maintain a reasonable life through the help of international aid."[190] Thus the West Bank is being driven to the same level of poverty as the Gaza Strip.

By July 2002, as I write this chapter, Israel's "separation" can no longer be compared to the apartheid of South Africa. As Ronnie Kasrils, South Africa's minister of water affairs, said in an interview with *Al Ahram Weekly:* "The South African apartheid regime never engaged in the sort of repression Israel is inflicting on the Palestinians. For all the evils and atrocities of apartheid, the government never sent tanks into black towns. It never used gunships, bombers, or missiles against the black towns or Bantustans. The apartheid regime used to impose sieges on black towns, but these sieges were lifted within days."[191] Nor, we may add, had South Africa applied a systematic policy of bringing the black population to starvation. What we are witnessing in the occupied territories—Israel's penal colonies—is the invisible and daily killing of the sick and wounded who are deprived of medical care, of the weak who cannot survive in the new poverty conditions, and of those who are approaching starvation.

Information has begun accumulating regarding the horrible conditions the Palestinians have been driven to. Even the U.S. ambassador to Israel, Daniel Kurtzer, is alarmed. "Krutzer told the Israeli authorities this week [late July 2002] that the situation in the occupied territories was 'a humanitarian disaster.'"[192] Earlier, at the annual dinner of the Wharton and Harvard Business School Clubs of Israel, Kurtzer told the audience that "the United Nations Office for the Coordination of Humanitarian Affairs (OCHA) reports that approximately two million Palestinians, or 62 percent of the population, are considered 'vulnerable,' meaning that they have had inadequate access to food, shelter, or health services. This figure is 25 percent higher than only six months ago." He also reported that "Initial findings from a USAID [U.S. Agency for International Development] funded study indicate that malnutrition among Palestinian children, defined as the stunting of growth or abnormally low body weight, is rising. A large percentage of children under five and women of childbearing age suffer from anemia."[193] More details on these initial findings were provided by *Ha'aretz:* "The researchers found that 9.3 percent of Palestinian children in the territories suffer from a temporary form of malnutrition while 13.2 percent of children are chronically under-nourished. The situation on the Gaza Strip is manifestly worse than that of the West Bank: While

3.5 percent of children on the West Bank suffer from chronic malnutrition, the figure for Gaza is 17.5 percent. The study concludes that these malnutrition statistics warrant classification (according to standards used by health officials) as a 'humanitarian emergency,' particularly in the Gaza Strip."[194]

Pushing the Palestinians to starvation is not just a tragic outcome of Israel's "war against terror." It is a systematic policy that, as we saw in Chapter V, Israel imposed right from the start of its present round of oppression, and which it has intensified gradually. It is a well-calculated strategy of ethnic cleansing.

At the same time that Israel deprives the Palestinians of their means of income, it also makes a substantial effort to diminish or block international aid, under the pretext that the aid is used to support terrorists and their families. At the outset of its new "operation" in June, Israel "decided to stop the flow of food aid and medicine from Iran and Iraq to Palestinians in the territories."[195] Iranian and Iraqi aid is an easy target for Israel, as these countries belong to President Bush's "axis of evil." However, Israel started launching a more ambitious campaign: The EU, the largest PA donor, is under constant pressure from Israel to cut its aid, which is used, inter alia, to pay the salaries of teachers and health workers. The tactics are always the same: Israel provides some documents presumably linking the PA to terror. Any aid to the PA is, therefore, aid to terror. Thus, "in the shadow of the Israeli accusations, the European Parliament's budgetary committee last week [early June 2002] delayed the transfer of 18.7 million euros in financial aid to the PA until the EC [European Commission] reports how the money is to be distributed...."[196] That amount was eventually transferred, but the EU remains under pressure to reduce its aid.

UNRWA's aid was Israel's next target. UNRWA—the UN Relief and Works Agency for Palestinians in the Near East—has become a major source of food for Palestinians in the besieged territories. As we saw in Chapter VI, its food supplies are now delivered not only to the refugee camps, but also to towns and villages. The amount of food UNRWA supplies has increased fourfold in the first year of the Palestinian uprising,[197] and much more since then. By the end of June 2002, "Israel [has begun] a campaign in the United States and the United Nations to urge a reconsideration of the way the UN Relief and Works Agency, which runs the Palestinian refugee camps in the West Bank and Gaza, operates. Israel charges that UNRWA workers simply ignored the fact that Palestinian organizations were turning the camps into terrorist bases and it is demanding the agency start reporting all military or terrorist actions within the camps to the UN.... Meanwhile, Jewish and pro-Israeli lobbyists in the U.S. are waging a parallel campaign... American Jewish lobbyists are basing their efforts on the fact that the U.S. currently contributes some 30 percent of UNRWA's $400 million a year budget, and is therefore in a position to influence the agency: A congressional refusal to approve UNRWA's funding could seriously disrupt its operations."[198] That campaign was not yet openly demanding cutting UNRWA's aid and presence altogether, but raising the impossible demand that UNRWA should serve as an active force in "the war against terror" ("reporting military or terrorist actions") is the first step toward such a demand.[199]

As we have seen, since September 11, Sharon has been constructing an analogy between the occupied territories and Afghanistan, between the PA and Al Qaeda. Sharon keeps declaring that the solution to Palestinian terror, and the required reforms, should be along the lines set in Afghanistan. The analogy is frighteningly revealing: As it established reforms in Afghanistan, the U.S. forced starvation upon millions of people. This is how Noam Chomsky has described it:

On Sept. 16, the *New York Times* reported that "Washington has also demanded [from Pakistan] a cutoff of fuel supplies...and the elimination of truck convoys that provide much of the food and other supplies to Afghanistan's civilian population." Astonishingly, that report elicited no detectable reaction in the West, a grim reminder of the nature of the Western civilization that leaders and elite commentators claim to uphold—yet another lesson that is not lost among those who have been at the wrong end of the guns and whips for centuries.... In the following days, those demands were implemented.... "The country was on a lifeline," one evacuated aid worker reports, "and we just cut the line." (*New York Times Magazine*, September 30, 2001.) According to the world's leading newspaper, then, Washington demanded that Pakistan ensure the death of enormous numbers of Afghans, millions of them already on the brink of starvation, by cutting off the limited sustenance that was keeping them alive.[200]

Arundhati Roy's summary of the situation in Afghanistan at the time seems painfully applicable to what the Palestinians are enduring: "Witness the infinite justice of the new century. Civilians starving to death while they're waiting to be killed."[201]

CHAPTER IX

WHAT DOES ISRAEL REALLY WANT?

As we saw, the destruction of the Palestinian Authority and the moves to topple Arafat were not spontaneous reactions to terrorism, but the realization of a precalculated plan. But what is the rationale behind this systematic drive to eliminate the institutional structures formulated following the Oslo Accords, and reestablish full military rule in the occupied territories? It certainly cannot be based on "disappointment" with Arafat's performance, as has been endlessly repeated. The fact of the matter is that from the perspective of Israel's interests in maintaining the occupation, Arafat has been fulfilling Israel's expectations for years.

ARAFAT'S SECURITY RECORD

As far as Israeli security goes, there is nothing further from the truth than the false accusations presented in the White Book (discussed in Chapter VII) and subsequent Israeli propaganda. To take just one example, in 1997—the year mentioned in the White Book as an instance of when Arafat gave a "green light to terror"—a "security agreement" was signed between Israel and the Palestinian Authority, under the auspices of the CIA's Tel Aviv station chief, Stan Muskovitz. Clause 1 of the agreement committed the Palestinian Authority to take active care of the security of Israel—to fight "the terrorists, the terrorist base, and the environmental conditions leading to support of terror" in cooperation with Israel, including "mutual exchange of information, ideas, and military cooperation." Clause 13 of the agreement committed the Palestinian Authority "to take all necessary security steps to penetrate the terror organizations and act to destroy them from the inside."[202] Arafat's security services carried out this job faithfully, with assassinations of Hamas terrorists (disguised as "accidents") and periodic arrests of Hamas political leaders.

Let us follow just one of these cases in detail—the assassination of the Hamas terrorist Muhi A-Din A-Sherif in March 1998, since it is a useful illustration of the way the Palestinian Authority has operated and of its relations with the Israeli secret services.[203] The PA's cooperation on A-Sherif's case started at the end of December 1997. At that time Roni Shaked reported in *Yediot Aharonot* that the Israeli security forces arrested Abdalla Al-Bakri, in whose Al-Bira home A-Sherif was hiding. The information obtained in his interrogation was passed on to the

Palestinian forces, and they carried out a raid of the house. A-Sherif managed to escape before they arrived.[204]

Based on the many pieces of information that appeared in the Israeli media, it is possible to obtain a pretty clear picture of what happened next. At the end of March 1998, Gibril Rajub's Palestinian "preventive security" forces had finally managed to arrest A-Sherif. They interrogated him, most likely using heavy torture. Then they executed him. To cover up traces of their crime, on March 29, at 9 P.M., they staged an explosion in a garage near Ramallah where his body was later found. Based on the information the security forces obtained from A-Sherif during his interrogation, that same day they arrested several Hamas activists who had been in touch with him, including Rasan Adasi, a student at Bir Zeit University. There is no evidence that Israeli forces were physically involved at any stage of this operation.

In Israel, the event was warmly greeted. In a meeting with Arafat on April 3, 1998, Ami Ayalon—then head of the Security Service (Shin Bet)—publicly thanked Arafat for his help in preventing terrorist bombings.[205] In a government meeting on April 5, 1998, Ayalon announced that "Arafat is doing his job—he is fighting terror and puts all his weight against Hamas."[206]

However, in the occupied territories, news about the Palestinian Authority's role could have been explosive, particularly if the truth about murdering a Palestinian detainee after interrogation came out. It seems that the original intention was to present the event as an accident that took place while preparing bombs. This is the common cover-up used in previous Israeli-Palestinian "elimination" operations, as in the case of Kamal Kahil, killed in an explosion in Gaza's Sheik-Raduan in April 1995. The same practice is still used frequently for Israeli assassinations that the military wishes to hide. But things got out of hand when the Palestinian Authority pathologist Dr. Jalal Jaabri told A-Sherif's family that he had found bullets in his body, indicating that A-Sherif's was killed prior to the explosion. For a day or two, while working on an alternative cover-up, Gibril Rajub was spreading rumors that it was Israeli security forces who killed A-Sherif, and then brought his body to the garage in Ramallah.

Finally, Rajub found a solution, familiar from the colonially ruled banana republics. In a press conference on April 4, 1998, he announced that it was A-Sherif's own organization, Az-ad-din al-Kassem (the military wing of Hamas), that killed him. The specific version on that day (destined to change many times since) was that the murderer was Aadel Awdalla, head of the organization in the West Bank, and that his motive was based on a power conflict over leadership. Rajub even provided as "evidence" a written confession from Rasan Adasi (detained the day of the explosion), who presumably took part in the planning, and witnessed the whole thing, together with two other Hamas activists who, miraculously, were also detained the same day.[207] We probably can't know if the nineteen-year-old Adasi was tortured, as Hamas sources said, or if he agreed to a deal to save him-

Tanya Reinhart

self from a fate similar to A-Sherif's. (His lawyer was not allowed to meet him.) In any case, Adasi's written confession is the only evidence for this absurd plot. In the days that followed, the motives kept changing daily, and the major suspect changed as well, from Aadel Awdalla to his brother, Imad, who got arrested. (In the end, both brothers were assassinated a few months later by Israeli undercover units near Hebron, based on information provided by the Palestinian security services.)

Israeli security sources initially expressed skepticism toward the new development. The seams appeared too loose, and it looked like the story could not possibly pass in even a semi-free society. "The Palestinian Authority is making a dangerous move. Tomorrow someone will want to talk to the detainee that confessed, and verify his version," said a source to *Ha'aretz*.[208] *Ha'aretz* also pointed out that in the history of Hamas, there has never been an internal execution over any conflict, except for those accused of collaboration. The security sources recommended sticking to the original story of an accident involving explosives. As for the pathologist's devastating evidence, the Israelis proposed that the Palestinians claim that there were bullets in the car which accidentally discharged directly into A-Sherif's chest during the accidental explosion.[209] Bullets, at least, can't talk.

But under the tyrannical rule that Arafat and his gang have established in the territories, any story can be sold. Every attempt to reach the truth is brutally silenced. Dr. Jaabri, the Palestinian Authority's official pathologist, was fired and arrested, and released a statement denying his previous findings. Dr. Abdel Azis Al Rantisi, the Hamas political leader who hinted in an interview with the *Jerusalem Post* at the role of Rajub in the affair, was subsequently called in for investigation, and on April 9, 1998, he was arrested. The Palestinian journalist who interviewed him was forced to publish a denial—just like in the days of Stalin's Soviet Union. The Palestinian press can only print what the Palestinian Authority approves of, and just to make sure nothing undesirable leaked to the foreign press, the Reuters office in Gaza was closed for three months, and the five Palestinian stringers for Reuters were detained until they signed an obligation "not to cause fanatic unrest."[210]

During this time, Israeli "security sources" were calling on Arafat to expand his crackdown of the civil sections of Hamas, and reminded him of the clause in the security agreement that required destroying the "environmental conditions," i.e., the social infrastructure and the political opposition, not just the military sections. The Palestinian Authority responded by conducting a wave of arrests of Hamas political leaders. "I am pleased with the process that started," said then Israeli Defense Minister Itchak Mordechai.[211]

This is just one case study. Ample information has been published in the Israeli media regarding similar activities of Arafat's security forces, and Israeli "security sources" were at the time full of praises for Arafat's achievements. The rate of success of Israeli security forces in containing terrorism was never higher than Arafat's; in fact, it was much lower. Dr. Boaz Ganor, a security expert from the Interdisciplinary Center in Herzliyah, explained the security concept that underlies the Oslo agreements: "At the basis of the conception was the idea of reliance upon the Palestinian intelligence capabilities, especially since in 1993 they were vastly superior to our [intelligence capabilities] as occupiers. This is a system that lives within its people, is familiar with it, and receives cooperation from it."[212]

In left and critical circles, one can hardly find compassion for Arafat's personal fate (as opposed to the tragedy of the Palestinian people). As David Hirst wrote in the *Guardian*, when Arafat returned to the occupied territories in 1994, "he came as collaborator as much as liberator. For the Israelis, security—theirs, not the Palestinians'—was the be-all and end-all of Oslo. His job was to supply it on their behalf. But he could only sustain the collaborator's role if he won the political quid pro quo which, through a series of 'interim agreements' leading to 'final status,' was supposedly to come his way. He never could.... [Along the road] he acquiesced in accumulating concessions that only widened the gulf between what he was actually achieving and what he assured his people he would achieve, by this method, in the end. He was Mr. Palestine still, with a charisma and historical legitimacy all his own. But he was proving to be grievously wanting in that other great and complementary task, building his state-in-the-making. Economic misery, corruption, abuse of human rights, the creation of a vast apparatus of repression—all these flowed, wholly or in part, from the Authority over which he presided."[213]

But from the perspective of the Israeli occupation, all this means that the Oslo plan was, essentially, successful. Arafat did manage, through harsh means of oppression, to contain the frustration of his people and guarantee the safety of the settlers, as Israel continued to build new settlements and appropriate more Palestinian land. The oppressive machinery—Arafat's various security forces—were formed and trained in collaboration with Israel. Much energy and resources were put into building this complex Oslo apparatus. It is often admitted that Israeli security forces cannot manage to prevent terror any better than Arafat can. Why, then, were the military and political echelon so determined to destroy all this in October 2000, even before the waves of terrorism started? Answering this requires a look at history.

THE TWO POLES IN ISRAEL'S POLITICS

Ever since the 1967 occupation, Israeli military and political elites have deliberated over the question of how to keep maximum land with minimum Palestinian population.

The leaders of the "1948 generation"—Yigal Alon, Moshe Dayan, Yitzhak Rabin, Sharon, and Peres—were raised on the myth of the "redemption of land." The myth, which every Israeli of that generation grew up with, was that the land that once belonged to the Jewish people should be "redeemed" and saved, namely, taken back from its alien residents. This can be achieved through both patient purchasing and appropriation of the land bit by bit, or, if necessary, through war. Sharon, in a surprisingly candid interview in April 2001 offered a glimpse into the worldview formed in the Palm'ah ("striking forces"), the pre-state military legion whose thinking has since dominated the Israeli military system. In this worldview, everything is entangled into one romantic framework: the fields, the blossoms of the orchards, the plough, and the wars. The heart of this ideology is the sanctity of the land. "When Sadat would tell me that for the Arabs land is sacred, that made me envious," Sharon confessed. "People today don't get so excited by the idea of 'another acre and another acre' [of land]. But I still get excited." In Sharon's vision, land should be fought for forever. "The War of Independence has not ended," and will, perhaps, go on forever. "A normal people does not ask questions like 'will we always live by the sword' […] the sword is part of life."[214]

In a 1976 interview, Moshe Dayan, who was the defense minister in 1967, explains what led to the decision to attack Syria in the war of 1967. In the collective Israeli consciousness of the period, Syria was conceived as a serious threat to the security of Israel, and a constant initiator of aggression toward the residents of northern Israel. But according to Dayan, this was "bullshit"—Syria was not a threat to Israel before 1967. "Just drop it," he said as an answer to a question about the northern residences. "I know how at least 80 percent of all the incidents with Syria started. We were sending a tractor to the demilitarized zone and we knew that the Syrians would shoot. If they did not shoot, we would instruct the tractor to go deeper, till the Syrians finally got upset and started shooting. Then we employed artillery, and later also the air force.... I did that...and Yitzhak Rabin did that, when he was there (as commander of the Northern front, in the early sixties)."[215]

According to Dayan, what led Israel to provoke Syria this way was the greediness for the land—the idea that it was possible "to grab a piece of land and keep it, until the enemy gets tired and gives it to us." The Syrian land was, as he says, particularly tempting, since, unlike Gaza and the West Bank, it was not heavily populated. Dayan insisted that the decision to attack Syria in 1967 was not motivated by security reasons. "The Syrians, on the fourth day of the war, were not threatening us." He adds that the decision was also influenced by a delegation sent to Prime Minister Levi Eshkol by the northern kibbutzes, "who did not even try to hide their greed of that land."[216]

The 1967 war brought Israel much land (and water). Israel gained control over the Syrian Golan Heights, the West Bank, Gaza, and the Sinai Peninsula (which it returned to Egypt in 1982). As in Dayan's description, the lightly populated Golan Heights was an easy target for annexation. Ninety percent of its 100,000 residents fled or were expelled during the war, and the settlements Israel started building met little opposition.[217] On December 14, 1982, the Knesset passed a law extending Israeli civilian law and administration to the Golan Heights—in effect, annexing the land.

But the West Bank and Gaza posed a problem. The simple solution of annexing these lands to Israel would entail turning the occupied Palestinians into Israeli citizens. In the case of the Golan Heights, the remaining Syrian residents indeed received Israeli citizenship, but applying the same offer to the densely populated West Bank and Gaza would have caused what has been labeled in Israeli political discourse "the demographic problem"—fear that a Jewish majority could not be sustained. Therefore, two basic approaches were developed.

The Alon plan of the Labor Party, which was discussed briefly in Chapter II, proposed annexation of 35 to 40 percent of the territories to Israel, and either Jordanian rule, or some form of self-rule for the rest of the land on which the Palestinians actually lived. Thus, in an 1983 interview, Rabin stated, "I say now that we are ready to give back roughly 65 percent of the territory of the West Bank and the Gaza strip, where over 80 percent of the population now resides."[218] In the eyes of its proponents, this plan represented a necessary compromise compared to the alternatives of either giving up the territories altogether, or eternal bloodshed (such as we witness today). They believed it was impossible to repeat the 1948 "solution" of mass expulsion, either for moral considerations, or because world public opinion would never allow it to happen again.

The second approach—which was always dominant in

military circles and whose primary spokesman was Ariel Sharon—assumed that, given Israel's military superiority, Palestinian resistance could eventually be broken. It is necessary, therefore, to break any form of Palestinian organization or power base, as Sharon did in Lebanon in 1982. In its extreme realization, this approach maintains that it should be possible to find more acceptable and sophisticated ways to achieve a 1948-style "solution." It would only be necessary to find another state for the Palestinians. "Jordan is Palestine" was the phrase that Sharon coined in the 1980's. From this point of view, future arrangements should guarantee that as many as possible of the Palestinians in the occupied territories would move to Jordan. For Sharon, this was part of a more global worldview, by which Israel could establish "new orders" in the region—a view which he experimented with through Israel's war with Lebanon.

At Oslo, it seemed that the Alon plan path triumphed. But in reality, both approaches were visible during the Oslo years. Right from the start of the Oslo process in September 1993, two conceptions were competing in the Israeli political and military system. One, advocated most notably by Yossi Beilin, was indeed striving to implement some version of the Alon plan. It appeared at least initially that Rabin was willing to follow this line. In return for Arafat's commitment to control Palestinian frustration and guarantee the security of Israel, Rabin would allow the Palestinian Authority to run the enclaves in which Palestinians still resided with some form of self-rule that could be called a

Palestinian "state." Gradually it became apparent to the proponents of the Alon plan that they could even extend the "Arab-free" areas beyond the 35 percent to which Rabin agreed in 1983. As we have seen, in practice the Palestinians have already been dispossessed of about 50 percent of their lands, which are now state lands, security zones, and "land reserves for the settlements." Labor circles began to talk of Oslo as the Alon Plus plan, namely, more land for Israel. However, it appeared that they would be satisfied with this 50 percent, and would allow Palestinian self-rule in the other 50 percent.

The competing view objected to giving even that much to the Palestinians. This was mostly visible in military circles, whose most vocal spokesman in the early years of Oslo was Ehud Barak, then the military chief-of-staff. Another center of opposition was, of course, Ariel Sharon and the extreme right wing, which was against the Oslo process from the start. The affinity between military circles and Sharon is hardly surprising. Sharon—the last of the generals of the 1948 generation—was a legendary figure in the army, and many of the younger generals were his disciples. We have observed already, in Chapter IV, some of the history of Barak and Sharon's cooperation. As Amir Oren wrote, "Barak and Sharon both belong to a line of political generals that started with Moshe Dayan."[219]

On the eve of Oslo, the majority of Israelis were tired of war. In their eyes, the fights over land and resources were over. Haunted by the memory of the Holocaust, most

Israelis believe that the 1948 War of Independence, with its horrible consequences for the Palestinians, was necessary to establish a state for the Jews. But now that they have a state, they just long to live normally on whatever land they have. However, the ideology of the "redemption of land" never died out in the army, or in the circle of political generals whose careers moved from the military to the government. In their eyes, Sharon's alternative of fighting the Palestinians to the bitter end and imposing new regional orders likely failed in Lebanon in 1982 because of the weakness of "spoiled Israeli society." But now, given the new war philosophy established through U.S. military operations in Iraq, Kosovo, and Afghanistan, the political generals believe that with Israel's massive military superiority, it might still be possible to "win" against the Palestinians and gain more land through the use of force.

While Sharon's party was in the opposition at the time of Oslo, Barak, as chief-of-staff, participated in the negotiations and played a crucial role in shaping the agreements and Israel's attitude to the Palestinian Authority. I quote from an article I wrote in February 1994, because it reflects what anybody who carefully read the Israeli media could see at the time:

> From the start, it has been possible to identify two
> Israeli conceptions that underlie the Oslo process.
> One is that it will reduce the cost of the occupation,
> using a Palestinian patronage regime, with Arafat as

the senior cop responsible for the security of Israel. The other is that the process should lead to the collapse of Arafat and the PLO. The humiliation of Arafat, and the amplification of his surrender, will gradually lead to loss of popular support. Consequently, the PLO will collapse, or enter power conflicts. Thus, the Palestinian society will lose its secular leadership and institutions.

In the power-driven mind of those eager to maintain the Israeli occupation, the collapse of the secular leadership is interpreted as an achievement, because it would take a long while for the Palestinian people to get organized again, and, in any case, it is easier to justify even the worst acts of oppression when the enemy is a fanatic Muslim organization.

Most likely, the conflict between the two competing conceptions is not settled yet, but at the moment, the second seems more dominant: In order to carry out the first, Arafat's status should have been strengthened, with at least some achievements that could generate support from the Palestinians, rather than Israel's policy of constant humiliation and breach of promises.[220]

Nevertheless, for those whose goal was the destruction of the Palestinian identity and the eventual Israeli redemption of Palestinian land, Oslo was a failure. The Palestinian

Authority never collapsed. Instead, Palestinian society continued to rely on its marvelous strategy of *sumud*—sticking to the land and sustaining the pressure. Right from the start, Hamas political leadership and other Palestinian organizations warned that Israel was trying to push the Palestinians into a civil war in which they would slaughter one another. All sectors of Palestinian society cooperated to prevent this danger, and to defuse conflicts when they started deteriorating into armed clashes. They also managed, despite the tyranny of Arafat's rule, to build an impressive number of institutions and infrastructures. The Palestinian Authority does not consist only of corrupt rulers and various security forces: The elected Palestinian council, which operates under endless restrictions, is still a representative political framework, and a basis for future democratic institutions.

In 1999, the army got back to power through the political generals—first Barak, and then Sharon. (They collaborated in the 2001 elections to guarantee that no other civil candidate would have a chance to run.) The road was thus open to correcting what they viewed as the grave mistake of Oslo. As we saw in Chapter IV, in order to get there, it was first necessary to convince the spoiled Israeli society that the Palestinians were not willing to live in peace and were threatening Israel's very existence. Sharon alone could not have possibly achieved that, but Barak did succeed with his "generous offer" fraud. After Barak and a year of horrible Palestinian terror attacks, combined with massive Israeli propaganda and lies, Sharon and the military felt that the road was open for the full execution of their plan.

Why is it so urgent for Sharon and the military to topple Arafat? Shabtai Shavit, former head of the Mossad (Israel's foreign intelligence agency) who is no longer bound by restraints posed on "official sources," explains: "In the thirty-something years that he [Arafat] has ruled, he managed to reach real achievements in the political and international sphere.... He got the Nobel Peace Prize, and in a single phone call, he can obtain a meeting with any leader in the world. There is nobody in the Palestinian gallery that can enter his shoes in this context of international status. If they [the Palestinians] will lose this gain, for us, this would be a huge achievement. The Palestinian issue will vanish from the international agenda."[221] The goal is thus to eliminate the Palestinians from the international agenda so the job of ethnic cleansing can continue undisturbed.

It is hard to avoid the conclusion that behind the rhetoric that at times suggests otherwise, the creation of a real Palestinian state on land from which all Israeli military forces have fully withdrawn is not even considered a remote option in the military-political circles ultimately making such decisions. After thirty-five years of occupation, the two options competing in the Israeli power system are precisely the same as those set by the generation of 1948: apartheid (the Alon-Oslo plan), or "transfer" (the historical Sharon plan)—mass evacuation, as happened in 1948.

THE RULE OF THE MILITARY

In assessing the dangers ahead, the role of the military in Israeli politics deserves special attention. During the Oslo years, it seemed that the conflict between the two conceptions outlined above also existed in the army. Thus, Amnon Shahak, who replaced Barak as chief-of-staff, was known as a supporter of the Oslo process. The same is true of Ami Ayalon, then head of the Security Service, who openly came out with critical views of Israeli policies after he retired, and who is currently a leading voice in the call for immediate Israeli withdrawal from the occupied territories. But gradually such voices have been silenced.

A dominant figure that emerged during the Oslo years is Major General Moshe Ya'alon, who is also known for his connections with the settlers. As head of the Military Intelligence (Am'an) between 1995 and 1998, Ya'alon confronted then chief-of-staff Amnon Shahak and consolidated the anti-Oslo line that now dominates the Military Intelligence view. Contradicting the position of Ayalon and the Security Service (Shin Bet), which, as we saw, praised the security cooperation between Israel and the Palestinian Authority, Ya'alon claimed in a cabinet meeting in September 1997, and also later, that "Arafat is giving a green light to terror."[222] During Barak's days in office, Ya'alon became one of his closest confidants on the small military team that Barak assembled to work with.[223] Barak appointed him deputy chief-of-staff at the outset of the current

Tanya Reinhart

Palestinian uprising, and in 2002, Sharon appointed him chief-of-staff.

As we saw in Chapter V, the Israeli army has been eager and ready from the start of the current escalation, not only with all military means, but also with political plans and propaganda themes. In November 2000, Guy Bechor, a senior security analyst at *Yediot Aharonot* wrote: "Day after day, we read in the press assessments by IDF Intelligence about Arafat's status as a partner, the utility or futility of continuing talks with him, attacking or holding back an attack on the PA. It is doubtful that the army has a mandate to deal with these kinds of political issues but, in any case, the IDF presents a clear thesis here: Arafat initiated the wave of riots, he controls them absolutely, with the push of a button he can stop them. Deputy Chief of Staff Maj. Gen. Moshe Ya'alon even openly jeered at anyone thinking otherwise."[224]

Israeli military and political systems have always been closely intertwined. According to a U.S. "congressional source," "In Israel, unlike the United States, the setting of national strategies and priorities is a consensus issue, not carried out by bodies headed by political appointees, but by men in uniform.... All previous Israeli governments have given 'a tremendous amount of attention' to suggestions by the military because they represent the 'permanent government,' this source said."[225] Still, the army has never had such a dominant role in Israeli politics as it has had since the period of Barak and as it now has under Sharon. It is often apparent that the real decisions are made by the military rather than the political echelon. This is visible even externally. In all televised coverage of meetings of the Israeli government or cabinet, one sees at least an equal number of uniformed representatives of the various branches of the military and the security forces. Military seniors brief the press (they capture at least half of the news space in the Israeli media), and brief and shape the views of foreign diplomats; they go abroad on diplomatic missions, outline political plans for the government, and express their political views on any occasion.[226]

Guy Bechor continued, in the same article from early November 2000:

> When the prime minister is also the defense minister and there is no healthy dialogue between them as there should be; when cabinet meetings take place at the Defense Ministry; when ministers say *amen* to almost any military whim, the outcome can be disastrous.... The press should play a balancing civilian role, but in its patriotic attitude, it is usually a military choir.... The government and the decision-makers, the Knesset, the press, the State Attorney's Office and the other civil and economic institutions follow the military piper from Hamlyn. Not that there are no exceptions, but that is what they are—exceptions....
>
> It should be hoped that the militarization process that is taking over our agenda can be curbed, and

that the army retreats to its natural position. But before that, all the civil institutions must take up their roles again: the government as a molder and not a follower of policy, the Knesset as a critical factor, the State Attorney's Office charged with the civil interpretation of the rule of law, and the media as a factor that uses rational thought, and the general public in contributing its common sense.[227]

No one, of course, took this advice, and military dominance in Israel has only become more deeply established during Sharon's time in office. The army, particularly the previous Chief-of-Staff Shaul Mofaz, occasionally got into vocal public clashes with the political system, even with Sharon, whom, despite all his "glorious" past, the military echelon considers a bit outdated. One such big clash was in October 2001, when Sharon—pressed by the U.S. to go more slowly—required that the army temporarily withdraw from the Abu-Snina area in Hebron, which it had entered after the assassination of right-wing Israeli tourism minister Rehavam Zeevi. But Mofaz refused to withdraw because "he knew we [will] get back there…according to the comprehensive military plans."[228]

It was reported that a further source of conflict between the military and the government has been the military's insistence that Arafat should be assassinated and not just removed from power.[229] This is something that the U.S. has not approved of, so neither Barak nor Sharon has agreed to that so far. Journalist Richard Sale, in an article quoted above, report-ed that "what worries Washington policy makers is that Mofaz last November [2000] led a rebellious party of Israeli generals, who wanted 'harsher measures' taken against the Palestinian insurgents, including assassinating the president of the Palestine Authority, Yassar Arafat, according to U.S. government officials. One U.S. congressional source described the blowout as 'the most severe crisis of civilian authority in the history of Israel.' This source explained the conflict cen-tered on 'the extent of the government's ability to disregard the Israeli defense establishment and the estimates of intelli-gence chiefs in the pursuit of policy.'"[230]

The military is the most stable—and most dangerous—political factor in Israel, one that will remain in power long after Sharon falls. As Amir Oren put it, Mofaz is wrongly perceived as "someone who prefers Likud to Labor. In fact...he does not care who is the prime minister and the defense minister, as long as they don't last long in their office. In the last six years, since October 1995, there were five prime ministers and six defense ministers, but only two chiefs-of-staff."[231]

As the military is the driving force behind Israel's poli-tics, it is appropriate to wonder what it really wants. What can it have in mind as a replacement to the Oslo arrange-ments? The present declared goal is to reinstitute Israel's military rule in the occupied territories. But as we saw, the Oslo arrangements were conceived precisely because the military occupation no longer worked. The burden of polic-

Tanya Reinhart

ing the territories was much too heavy on the army, the reserves, and Israeli society, and the IDF's success in preventing terrorism turned out to be, in fact, much lower than that of the Palestinian Authority in later years. No matter how "successful" Israel's present operations are, as long as the occupation continues, Palestinian resistance will continue as well, and as everyone knows, nothing can stop desperate people from turning to desperate means—terrorism. After the Lebanon experience, and after the seven years of Oslo, during which Israeli society got used to the idea that the occupation could continue at no cost, with the Palestinian Authority taking care of the settlers' security, it is hard to imagine that anyone believes that Israel can revert to a pre-Oslo situation as a long-term solution.

A serious danger that should not be ignored is that the political generals really mean it when they speak about "the second half of 1948." They may believe that under the appropriate conditions of regional escalation, it would be possible to execute the transfer option—the mass evacuation of the Palestinian residents, as happened in 1948 (Sharon's old vision that Jordan is the Palestinian state).

Indeed, the transfer idea is plainly on the table in Israeli political discourse. What was until a short while ago the lunatic right wing of the Rehavam Zeevi school is now becoming Israel's political center. In March 2001, *Ha'aretz* reported on a conference at the Interdisciplinary Center in Herzliyah of about three hundred "prominent personalities from the core of Israel's political and defense establishment"—the center of the center. The conclusions of the forum were solemnly presented to the president of Israel, and what the participants suggested was the transfer solution: "It will be necessary to find some place for resettlement outside the State of Israel (perhaps to the east of the Jordan river) for the Palestinian population of the territories." Israeli Palestinians would be deprived of their citizenship by "transferring them to Palestinian sovereignty." The state's resources should be invested in "fostering quality," that is, in the "strong population" and not in the "non-Zionist population," which includes "Arabs, ultra-orthodox Jews and foreign workers," whose natural increase is a source of concern.[232]

The danger of transfer may seem far-fetched. Unlike the daily ethnic cleansing that Israel has been carrying out, a full-scale evacuation with masses of refugees would not be simple to carry out, even in the current climate set by the U.S. global war on terrorism. The only way it could become feasible is under the umbrella of an extensive regional war. However, some evidence actually suggests that Israel has been preparing for such a war, and is awaiting U.S. approval.

Many voices in the Arab world have warned for quite a while that Israel is preparing for war with Syria. Since September 11, Israeli military and diplomatic delegations have been openly lobbying the U.S. to extend the war to targets on the Israeli agenda. One such target—Iran—is already included in the U.S. axis of evil. But Israel has also pushed for

Tanya Reinhart

the inclusion of Syria. In another conference at the Herzliyah center in December 2001, Major General Uzi Dayan, one of the participants in these Israeli delegations to the U.S. "identified what he called the appropriate targets for the next stage of the global campaign: 'The Iran, Iraq and Syria triangle, all veteran supporters of terror that are developing weapons of mass destruction.' He said that 'they must be confronted as soon as possible, and that is also understood in the United States. Hizbollah and Syria have good reason to worry about the developments in this campaign.'"[233]

Israel's eagerness to open a new front has apparently found a willing ear in the U.S. hawks, particularly in the circles of Defense Secretary Donald Rumsfeld and his deputy Paul Wolfowitz. For U.S. hawks who push to expand the war against terror to Iraq and elsewhere, Israel is a real asset. There are few regimes in the world as eager as Israel to risk the life of its citizens for some new regional war. By the end of September 2001, the British *Observer* had already reported that "the plans put [by Rumsfeld] before the President during the past few days involve expanding the war beyond Afghanistan to include similar incursions by special operations forces—followed by air strikes by the bombers they would guide—into Iraq, Syria and the Beqaa Valley area of Lebanon, where the Syrian-backed Hizbollah (Party of God) fighters that harass Israel are based."[234]

So far, of course, these are just plans representing one pole in U.S. politics, but according to the Israeli press, concrete pressure on Syria began in December 2001. "U.S. officials have informed the Syrian and Lebanese governments in recent days that they must stop playing host to terror organizations. According to information that has reached Israel's security establishment, as the final stages in the Afghanistan war effort draw near, the Americans intend to step up pressure against the activity of terror organizations in Syria and Lebanon. U.S. emissaries visited Damascus and Beirut last week, and submitted their country's demands."[235]

By the summer of 2002, plans to attack Syria under the cover of a U.S. offensive against Iraq were openly discussed in the Israeli media. Here is a typical example: "A senior General Headquarters officer, observing Damascus, said this week that Hezbollah, Syria, and Iran are trying to trap Israel in a 'strategic ambush' and that Israel has to evade that ambush by setting one of its own, under circumstances convenient to it. Those circumstances could be created during or near the end of an American offensive against Iraq."[236]

Long before September 11, analysts warned about the dangers of war in the Middle East—a region loaded with nonconventional weapons. Israel's course is currently directed by an all-powerful group of fanatical generals who keep their plans secret from even the full forum of the Israeli government. These are the generals who are authorized to unleash Israel's nuclear arsenal. This is not a risk the world should accept. As Alain Joxe said in *Le Monde:* "It is time for Western public opinion to take over and to compel the government to take a moral and political stand facing the foreseen disaster, namely a situation of permanent war against the Arab and Muslim people and states—the realization of the double fantasy of Bin Laden and Sharon."[237]

CHAPTER X

THE WAY OUT

By mid-2002, after a year and a half of bloodshed, there are some signs that the policy of Sharon and the military may reach a dead end. Resistance and opposition among the Israeli people are finally awakening. The general's route is facing difficulties reminiscent of the Israeli adventure in Lebanon—difficulties which eventually forced Israel to pull out of Southern Lebanon. As we shall see, a solution that is gaining some momentum in the polls in Israel is for Israel to unilaterally pull out, as it has done in Lebanon. But there is also a serious obstacle—the doves in the Israeli political system, led by Yossi Beilin, are not advocating withdrawal, but rather a return to negotiations.

Many in the awakening peace camp in Israel and abroad are now clinging to a new myth. Four months after the current escalation began, another round of negotiations took place in Taba, Egypt, from January 21 to 27, 2001. These talks were based on the parameters proposed by Clinton, and the new myth they generated was that during this round "the sides were never as close to agreement." Here is, for example, how Avi Shlaim, a professor of international relations at Oxford University, explains this new dream of peace: "On December 23 2000, President Bill Clinton presented his 'parameters' for a final settlement of the conflict. These parameters reflected the long distance he had traveled from the American bridging proposals tabled at Camp David towards meeting Palestinian aspirations. The new plan provided for an independent Palestinian state over the whole of Gaza and 94–96 percent of the West Bank (with some territorial compensation from Israel proper); Palestinian sovereignty over the Arab parts of Jerusalem, Israeli sovereignty over the Jewish parts; and a solution to the Palestinian refugee problem.... At Taba the two teams made considerable progress on the basis of the Clinton parameters and came closer to an overall agreement than at any other time in the history of this conflict. But by this time Clinton and Barak were on their way out and Sharon was on his way in."[238]

All we should do, within this myth, is pick up from there and finish up the small details left open. Is it really so? Let us examine in some detail what happened in Taba.

FALSE EXPECTATIONS, ROUND II–THE CLINTON PLAN (TABA)

The background for the Taba round of negotiations in January 2001 was political crisis in Israel. For reasons that still remain somewhat mysterious, Prime Minister Barak resigned from office, then, in a paradox typical of Israeli democracy, he ran again for the position, campaigning against Sharon. It was in this strange moment—while Israel was preparing for elections—that the Taba negotiations took place. Barak's constituency was middle and left voters, many of whom were furious at the way he treated the earlier negotiations and the Palestinian uprising. (Eventually, this segment of about 20 percent of the voters abstained from the elections, as an act of protest led by the Israeli Arabs, which is why Barak had no chance to be reelected.) It was this constituency that Barak was trying to appeal to with a new hope for peace. There was not even a serious attempt to hide the fact that these talks were part of the election campaign. "A senior source in Prime Minister Ehud Barak's office says the purpose of the Israeli-Palestinian marathon talks starting on Sunday at Taba is to neutralize the Israeli Left."[239]

It was clear from the start that the purpose of the talks was to produce some optimistic "statement for the press," a goal that was essentially obtained: "Ehud Barak sent the leaders of the Left—Shlomo Ben-Ami, Yossi Beilin and Yossi Sarid—to Taba, with the aim of attaining an 'endorsement' for his candidacy from the Palestinian Authority. The Palestinian embrace appears to be the key to waking left-wing and Arab voters from their slumber. The three emissaries succeeded in fulfilling their mission. They convinced Abu Ala and his colleagues to sign a declaration stating that the two sides 'have never been closer to reaching an agreement.'"[240]

Sending the doves of the left on this mission was not without risks, as they could have accidentally reached some real agreement at least on small local issues. Barak entrusted his confidant Gil'ad Sher to watch out for such potential slips: "Ehud Barak has let the weight of his hand be felt at the peace negotiations [in Taba]: *Ma'ariv* has discovered that during one of the meetings between the Israeli and Palestinian negotiating teams, the PM's bureau chief, attorney Gil'ad Sher, took advantage of Shlomo Ben-Ami's momentary absence to announce to the participants (who included every member of the Palestinian negotiating team) that proposals will be accepted only in his presence.... 'It is important to me that all of the participants here know that, from here on, every proposal here, or any other suggestion you receive, is not an official proposal by the Israeli government unless I am here and present when the proposal is made.' According to the witnesses, most of those present at the meeting were surprised at the PM's bureau chief's blunt words, causing consternation among the Palestinians. The development is testimony to...the determined decision made by Barak not to reach a settlement with the Palestinians in the time that is left until the elections."[241]

But there was no particular need to worry. Even Yossi Beilin declared that "any Taba agreement is not binding.... If an agreement is reached at the Taba talks, it will only be a reference point for whatever government is set up after the elections, and will not obligate it."[242]

Nevertheless, it's noticeable that the Taba negotiations

were registered in history as a significant breakthrough, a view advocated most notably by Beilin. In Taba, as we saw, the Israeli doves took the floor. It is interesting, therefore, to review what they were willing to offer in this noncommittal setting, when they knew that their proposals would be "non-binding anyway."

The basis for the negotiations was the Clinton parameters that captured the headlines at the end of December 2000. As is standard in the "peace negotiations," these parameters have no written documentation. "The president did not set out the ideas in writing. He preferred to dictate them to the sides, word by word."[243] However, judging by their description in the Israeli media, the parameters essentially parallel the original Beilin–Abu Mazen plan discussed in the first section of Chapter II. In all crucial aspects (some of which will be mentioned below) they are fully faithful to the Israeli position, and do not reflect any substantial changes from Clinton's proposals at Camp David. Nevertheless, both sides announced that they accepted the parameters in principle. For the Palestinians, this was the only option open, given Clinton's threats: "According to diplomatic and Palestinian sources, Clinton told Arafat: 'If you don't answer affirmatively to this proposal, it will be proof that you aren't interested in real peace. In such a situation, Ehud Barak will declare war on you—and we will support him.'"[244]

The Taba negotiations themselves also failed to produce any document except for a general declaration of progress.

(The negotiations ended earlier than planned, under Barak's order.) However, a year later, detailed documentation was disclosed, prepared by the EU Special Representative to the Middle East Process, Ambassador Miguel Moratinos, and his team, who were present at Taba at the time of the negotiations. The document was released after consultations with the Israeli and Palestinian negotiators. It has been acknowledged by both parties as being a relatively fair description of the outcome of the negotiations. The document was published in *Ha'aretz* on February 15, 2002. So it can serve as a fair basis for answering the question of what the Israeli doves were willing to offer. (Unless otherwise specified, all quotes below are from that document.)

For the first time, both sides presented maps of their territorial expectations. "The Palestinian side presented some illustrative maps detailing its understanding of Israeli interests in the West Bank." Israel's map got closer to the original Beilin–Abu Mazen plan (which Barak extended in Camp David). Israel offered to return 92 percent of the territories, where the rest consists of "6 percent annexation…and additional 2 percent of land under a lease arrangement." (Section 1.1.) The Palestinian map acknowledged "3.1 percent annexation [to Israel] in the context of a land swap." (Section 1.1.) We should note that while the map of the Israeli doves is not substantially different than what Israel proposed before, the Palestinian map represents a serious concession. The 3.1 percent the Palestinians were willing to give up is in the center of the West Bank—the heart of Palestinian society.

What they would get in return is some desert dunes in the south of Israel (Halutza), with no land contiguity to the West Bank, or even the Gaza Strip.

The debate on the issue of annexation centered around the concept of blocs. The 3.1 percent of the center of the West Bank that the Palestinians expressed willingness to concede were the areas of the settlements themselves. The Israeli doves insisted that the settlements to be annexed would form blocs, including the land between the settlements and the Palestinian neighborhoods on these lands. "The Palestinian side stated that blocks would cause significant harm to the Palestinian interests and rights, particularly to the Palestinians residing in areas Israel seeks to annex. The Israeli side maintained that it is entitled to contiguity between and among their settlements.... The Palestinian maps had a similar conceptual point of reference stressing the importance of a non-annexation of any Palestinian villages and the contiguity of the West Bank and Jerusalem." (Section 1.1.) Another area of dispute was expansion of the settlements. "The Israeli maps included plans for future development of Israeli settlements in the West Bank. The Palestinian side did not agree to the principle of allowing further development of settlements in the West Bank. Any growth must occur inside Israel." (Ibid.)

Regarding Jerusalem, there was no change since the previous round, except perhaps in matters of language. The negotiators used the terms "open city" and "Capital for two states" to describe the same proposal we examined in detail in Chapter II, in which the Palestinian "capital" is the village Abu-Dis, to be named Al-Quds: "The Israeli side accepted that the city of Jerusalem would be the capital of the two states: Yerushalaim, capital of Israel and Al-Quds, capital of the state of Palestine. The Palestinian side expressed its only concern, namely that East Jerusalem is the capital of the state of Palestine." (Section 2.3.) As so diplomatically put here, "the only" concern that the Palestinians had is that East Jerusalem, rather than the suburban village Abu-Dis, should be the capital of Palestine; so the issue of Jerusalem is still to be solved.

Regarding the right of return, there was no substantial change in the positions of the two sides, except that the disagreements were couched in a language emphasizing "much progress." As we saw, there are two issues here. The first is principled and symbolic; the second, more difficult issue, is the practical implementation of the right of return. The symbolic issue of "the narrative'" is a matter of principle for the Palestinians, with no independent practical consequences for Israel. As we reviewed earlier, the Palestinians expect Israel to recognize its responsibility for the creation of the refugee problem. But Barak insisted at Camp David that Israel is willing to share the efforts to rehabilitate the refugees, but it is not willing to take responsibility. This position is repeated in the Clinton parameters: "Israel, the president states, is willing to recognize the moral and material suffering caused as a result of the '48 war and the need to share in the international efforts to rehabilitate them."[245]

Thus, instead of recognizing Israel's responsibility, Clinton suggests recognizing the Palestinian suffering.

Even at the informal gathering at Taba, the negotiating Israeli doves were not able to offer the symbolic gesture of reconciliation. "The Israeli side put forward a suggested joint-narrative for the tragedy of the Palestinian refugees. The Palestinian side discussed the proposed narrative and there was much progress, although no agreement was reached in an attempt to develop a historical narrative in the general text." (Section 3.1.) On the other, practical matters, "both sides engaged in a discussion of the practicalities of resolving the refugee issue." The Israeli negotiators proposed that a slightly higher number of refugees be allowed to return to Israel than that which Barak proposed in Camp David, but still rejected all Palestinian claims for restitution of refugee property.

What is most striking about the Taba negotiations, as depicted in this long and detailed report of Moratinos, is not so much what is mentioned, but what is absent. There is hardly any reference to the central obstacle for a peace solution—the Israeli settlements scattered in the areas that are not designated to be formally annexed by Israel. As it has always been in the past, much was left here for "implication." "It was implied that the Gaza Strip will be under total Palestinian sovereignty, but details have still to be worked out. All settlements there will be evacuated. The Palestinian side claimed it could be arranged in 6 months, a timetable not agreed to by the Israeli side." (Section 1.2.) In fact, no

Tanya Reinhart

timetable that the Israeli doves would find feasible for the evacuation of the Gaza settlements is mentioned in the report. Regarding the Jordan Valley, there does appear to be willingness on the side of the Israeli doves to give up the settlements there and only maintain a military presence. However, that exhausts the discussion of settlements in the whole report.

As we saw in Chapter II, the real problem with the Beilin–Abu Mazen plan was the idea that the Israeli settlements can stay "under Palestinian sovereignty," which essentially entails keeping the situation as is, with some symbolic tokens of "statehood" given to the Palestinian enclaves. In the absence of any indication to the contrary, one has to conclude that Beilin still believed in Taba that this would be a workable solution.

In the spirit that characterizes Israeli "peace proposals," creative language provides the route to bypassing reality. One option that has been frequently raised is that the areas of the Israeli settlements will be "leased" from the Palestinian "state." As noted above, a 2 percent "lease" was how the doves thought to extend the area of the annexed blocks. But it was proposed for other areas as well. *Yediot Aharonot* analyst Nahum Barnea reported this idea as part of Clinton's parameters, which were the declared basis for the Taba negotiations: "Leasing is also an option (Palestinian sources mention an Israeli proposal to lease [the settlement] Kiryat Arba and the Jewish Quarter in Hebron, and perhaps the northern part of the Gaza Strip)."[246] (The

Palestinians argued, correctly, in response to the lease request in Taba "that the subject of lease can only be discussed after the establishment of a Palestinian state and the transfer of land to Palestinian sovereignty." (Section 1.1.) It is perhaps remotely imaginable for, say, France to propose leasing a certain French-speaking area from Belgium. But pretending that we are talking about similar situations is the essence of the hypocrisy in this Israeli proposal. A closer analogy would be if France demanded, at the same time, that its army is posted in Belgium to protect its citizens in the leased areas and secure the "French only" roads connecting them to Paris.

As a further glimpse into what kind of a state the Israeli doves envision for the Palestinians, we can examine the issue of Israel's borders with its Arab neighbors. One would think that an independent state has at least full control over its international borders. But Israel's proposal for the "final agreement" has yet to include such a concept. This has been a consistent area of dispute, as was acknowledged in the description of the Clinton parameters. "The sides did not reach agreement on supervision for Palestine's external borders with Jordan and Egypt. The Palestinians demand full control over the crossings. Israel demands invisible Israeli supervision or American supervision. Another problem is guarding the border with Jordan: would this be by Palestinian forces or international forces who would thwart the infiltration of would-be immigrants."[247] The prevailing impression of the dispute over the Palestinian right of return has been that it centered around the number of Palestinians allowed to return to Israel proper, but that the Palestinians would be free to absorb refugees in their own state. In fact, Israel also demands to have a permanent say on that issue. Hence it demands direct control on "thwart[ing] the infiltration of would-be immigrants."

The Israeli doves did not move an inch on this issue. Again, in the EU-Moratinos report, disagreements are couched in an optimistic language of hopes and expectations, but the bottom line is that this disagreement remains unresolved. "The Palestinian side was confident that Palestinian sovereignty over borders and international crossing points would be recognized in the agreement. The two sides had, however, not yet resolved this issue including the question of monitoring and verification at Palestine's international borders." (Section 4.7.)

What Israel offered in Taba, then, is essentially the same as what it has been offering before and after Oslo: preservation of the Israeli occupation within some form of Palestinian autonomy or self-rule. Everything that regards land, water (not even discussed in Taba), control of the borders, and many other aspects will remain under total Israeli control, but the Palestinians will be allowed symbolic tokens of "sovereignty," including even the permission to call their enclaves a "state," and Abu-Dis its "capital."

Nevertheless, there was still one significant difference between Taba and the Camp David negotiations. As we saw in Chapter II, what really sabotaged the Camp David negotiations was Barak's demand of an "end of conflict" declaration and the annihilation of the relevant UN resolutions. The Israeli doves retracted this demand and the sides restated the validity of these resolutions: "The two sides agreed that in accordance with the UN Security Council Resolution 242, the June 4, 1967, lines would be the basis for the borders between Israel and the state of Palestine." (Section 1.) They also reaffirmed the validity of UN Resolution 194 regarding the refugees' right of return: "Both sides suggested, as a basis, that the parties should agree that a just settlement of the refugee problem in accordance with the UN Security Council Resolution 242 must lead to the implementation of UN General Assembly Resolution 194." (Section 3.)

For the Palestinians, this is a significant achievement. It means that no matter what arrangements Israel manages to force on them, Palestinian demands for Israeli fulfillment of these UN resolutions still hold legally. So, in effect, whatever will be decided and signed, in the spirit of Taba, cannot be viewed as the final agreement, as long as these resolutions are not truly met. There is of course a contradiction between the mention of the June 4, 1967, border as a basis and Israel's intentions to immediately annex 6 percent of the Palestinian side of that border. In practice, this means that although the Palestinians would still have no access to these areas (along with about half of the rest of their occupied land), Israel's annexation would have no legal validity, just as its one-sided annexation of Jerusalem is not legal by international law, violating UN Resolution 242.

This is also an achievement for Yossi Beilin. As we saw, he objected to Barak's "end of conflict" demand, realizing that this was not something the Palestinians could accept. For Beilin, it was not as essential that there would ever be a "final agreement." As a pragmatist, he was interested in maintaining quiet for as long as possible, and if the only way to keep it was going to be with eternal negotiations and intermediate agreements, that was fine with him. Beilin represents the other (Alon plan) pole in Israeli politics—the route of eternal negotiations while preserving and advancing the situation in Israel's favor.

THE DEAD END OF ETERNAL NEGOTIATIONS

The essence of the vision of eternal negotiations is well reflected in a *Ha'aretz* editorial immediately after the Taba negotiations. *Ha'aretz*, like the majority of the "business community" in Israel, has been supporting the Labor Party in the elections for years. (This is based on understanding that the relative calm, as well as the easing of international and Arab pressure, that the negotiations provide, is a better setting for business than constant "unrest."[248]) Faithful to the original goal of the Taba negotiations, namely, returning voters on the left back to the Labor Party, *Ha'aretz* wrote, "True, Barak is unable to offer the voters a framework agreement to assess. But if Barak and his team remain in office, there is the glimmer of a hope for serious negotiations, including perhaps some Palestinian comprehension of the Israeli peace camp's own limits of flexibility. There is a world of difference between the substance of the discussions at Taba and Ariel Sharon's putative "peace plan," which leaves no room for any further talks."[249]

This is, indeed, a painfully accurate description of the only choices the Israeli political system has produced so far: No one inside the system is talking about immediate steps toward withdrawal, evacuation of settlements, or real peace. The choices are either a return to the road of endless negotiations, which can perhaps gain a few years of quiet, or the continuous bloodshed offered by Ariel Sharon, the other political generals, and the military. This is how the choices have been set and presented since Madrid and Oslo.

These are precisely the two poles in Israeli politics that were examined in Chapter IX: preservation of the present apartheid situation under the cover of negotiations, or ethnic cleansing and mass evacuation. If all we can do is select between these two choices, one can understand choosing the first. Apartheid, as horrible as it is, is better than massive ethnic cleansing, because it gives the Palestinians the chance of survival. Apartheid can eventually be defeated, with long struggle, as in South Africa. I confess that often in the dark months of Israel's brutality, when the ethnic cleansing pole seemed to be winning, I prayed that Beilin would manage to take us back to the road of apartheid. Nevertheless, the trap in this line of thinking is the idea that these are the only choices.

A prevailing explanation for why there has been no progress in negotiations all these years is that in Israeli society there exists no majority for sweeping concessions. Hence, the well-intended and dovish Israeli leaders have to restrain themselves and offer only what the majority can swallow. In fact, there is nothing further from reality than this claim. Since at least the early 1990's (1992–93), there has been a wide consensus in Israeli society that peace with the Palestinians and other Arab neighbors requires withdrawal from the occupied territories and evacuation of settlements. For many years before that (following the war with Lebanon in 1982 and the first Palestinian uprising), Israeli public opinion formed a clear pattern. About one third is firmly against the occupation and the settlements on moral and ideological grounds; another third believes in Israel's right over the whole land and supports the settlements; the middle third is people with no fixed ideological view on that matter—people whose sole concern is the ability to lead a normal life. In 1993, at the time of Oslo, the middle third joined the end-the-occupation camp. As we saw in Chapter I, two-thirds of Israelis supported Oslo in all polls, though it was conceived as leading to Israeli withdrawal and the evacuation of the settlements.

This majority has remained stable. In a poll from 1997, 60 percent were for dismantlement of the settlements in return for peace. Even more interesting were the responses to the question of what would those opposing the evacuation of settlements do in case of forced evacuation. Only 13 percent said they would try to actively oppose the evacuation, and of those, only 2 percent said they were willing to even consider armed struggle. This is certainly a minority that a democracy can impose its will on.[250] A similar percentage of over 60 percent supported withdrawal and evacuation of all of the Golan Heights settlements during the negotiations with Syria in 1999. (See Chapter III.)

Even during the current escalation, under the spirit of blood and revenge that has been dominating Israeli public discourse, the support for evacuation of settlements decreased only slightly. According to a poll published in Ha'aretz on July 4, 2001, 52 percent of Israeli Jews supported forceful evacuation of part of the settlements in a unilateral withdrawal; 40 percent supported the evacuation of *all* settlements. Some of the withdrawal supporters indeed got confused and paralyzed by the massive propaganda about the far-reaching concessions that Barak had supposedly offered and that the Palestinians rejected. But a process of sobering up has begun. By February 2002 only 38 percent opposed the evacuation of any settlements.[251]

An argument often used to demonstrate that the majority of Israelis are against concessions is the fact that they elected Sharon (and the previous right-wing candidate Benjamin Netanyahu). This is a misguided argument. The election situation in Israel is identical to that found in many countries in the Western world. For years now, there have always been two candidates with more or less the same agenda, so there has been no real choice. The ideological

Tanya Reinhart

thirds tend to vote blindly for the party closer to their ideology at the declarative level. But the middle third has no means of choosing between the two otherwise similar candidates and thus the results resemble those of flipping a coin—each candidate gets around 50 percent of the votes, with a very small margin deciding the outcome.

What has happened in Israel since the 1996 elections is that parts of the left third stepped out of the game and developed the blank ballot strategy—a form of political struggle against the system of pseudo-choice. In the 1996 race between Peres and Netanyahu, the call to vote blank came only from left circles, and 4 percent of the votes were blank, while Peres needed less than 1 percent to be elected.[252] In the elections of 2000, where the hated Barak was the only candidate against Sharon, 20 percent of the voters (relative to previous elections) abstained or voted blank. It is reasonable to conclude that the majority in Israel is simply not represented in the political system, as is the case in many other places.

Thus, it is not the Israeli people who hinder progress, but the Israeli political system, which has been working, in fact, against the will of the majority. To numb this majority, it has been necessary to keep alive the illusion that the occupation is about to end, and at the same time to convince the majority that this cannot possibly happen overnight. Negotiations are still needed to work out all the details. Since Oslo, the dream of peace has been replaced by the myth of negotiations. According to the Oslo myth, we are facing difficult and complex problems that require years, maybe generations, of negotiations. And until the whole deal is agreed upon, it is impossible to evacuate even one tiny settlement. This is how, despite wide support, actual withdrawal and evacuation seem further away every year. The mainstream "peace camp" in Israel (Beilin, the Meretz party, and Peace Now) has cooperated with this concept of endless negotiations during all the years of the Oslo process. It seems that its message has been that peace is a wonderful idea, just not now.

But this route has failed. Even if Arafat or his predecessors agree to resume never-ending negotiations, Israel has lost the faith of the Palestinians, who are no longer willing to listen to vague promises about a future that never materializes while they watch more and more of their land being taken by settlers.

IMMEDIATE ISRAELI WITHDRAWAL

For true negotiations to occur, Israel must first withdraw unilaterally—as it did in Lebanon. It is astounding how simple it would be to do this. Most of the occupied territories can be evacuated immediately, within two or three months. The only way out is to begin right now.

As we saw in detail in Chapter II, Barak intended to formally annex to Israel about 6 to 10 percent of the West Bank, where the large Israeli settlement blocs are, populated with about 150,000 residents. But the biggest fraud in Barak's

Camp David plan was the fate of the 90 percent of the West Bank that was supposedly earmarked to belong to the "Palestinian state." These lands are cut up by isolated Israeli settlements, which were purposely built in the midst of the Palestinian population to enable Israeli control of these areas in the future. These isolated settlements are now inhabited by about 40,000 Israeli settlers. Still, they control 40 percent of the land of the West Bank. As a result, two million Palestinians are crowded in enclaves that consist of about 50 percent of the West Bank.

Israel can and should immediately evacuate at least this 90 percent of the West Bank, along with the whole of the Gaza Strip. Many of the residents of the isolated Israeli settlements are speaking openly in the Israeli media about their wish to leave. It is only necessary to offer them reasonable compensation for the property they will be leaving behind. The rest are hard-core "land redemption" fanatics—a negligent minority that will have to accept the will of the majority. They can be evacuated forcefully, as was done in Yamit, on the eve of the peace agreement with Egypt. Following the evacuation of the settlements the complete and immediate withdrawal of the Israeli army from all its bases and outposts in these Palestinian territories could commence.

Such a withdrawal would still leave under debate the 6 to 10 percent of the West Bank with the large settlement blocs that cannot be evacuated overnight, as well as the issues of Jerusalem and the right of return. Negotiations will still be needed to resolve these problems. However, during such negotiations Palestinian society could begin to recover, to settle the lands that the Israelis evacuated, to construct democratic institutions, and to develop its economy based on free contacts with whomever it wants. Under these circumstances, it should be possible to conduct negotiations with mutual respect, and to address the core issue: What is the right way for two peoples who share the same land to jointly build their future?[253]

This plan should not be confused with the various "unilateral separation" proposals that call for freezing and preserving the situation in the West Bank, using the model of the Gaza Strip. They involve building fences around the Palestinian enclaves to "separate" them from the neighboring Israeli settlements, and from each other. As Ami Ayalon, a prominent proponent of the real unilateral withdrawal plan, said in an interview with *Le Monde:* "I do not like the word separation, it reminds me of South Africa. I favor unconditional withdrawal from the Territories…what needs to be done, urgently, is to withdraw from the Territories. And a true withdrawal, which gives the Palestinians territorial continuity [in the West Bank] linked to Gaza, open to Egypt and Jordan."[254]

Doubts regarding immediate withdrawal of this kind are sometimes also voiced by opponents of the occupation. They fear that the first withdrawal from Gaza and most of the West Bank would dictate a permanent two-state situation, without a solution to the crucial questions of Jerusalem and the right of return. However, I believe it would be a grave oversight to give up the concrete chance to get back much of the Palestinian lands now, in the hope that in the future one could get more. Whatever solution the two peoples arrive at in the future, it must be based on the Palestinians having land, resources, and the freedom to develop anyway. So the process of acquiring these basics should start now, regardless of the final vision.

This plan is now becoming realistic. Despite the declared "success" of the latest military oppression, it becomes clearer that Israeli military force against the Palestinians is not a solution. As in Lebanon, the price of the occupation is again becoming intolerable for the army and Israeli society, which also has to endure the terrible and unforgivable terror attacks of desperate Palestinians. The Israeli economy is on the verge of collapse, and it is not clear how long it can continue to pay the price of the occupation.

At the same time, an amazing and encouraging fact is that support for peace and reconciliation is still strong among the Palestinian people. A survey by the Development Studies Program at Bir Zeit University in the West Bank that was conducted in February 2002 found out that "77 percent believe that both Palestinians and Israelis have the right to live in peace and security. 73 percent find it necessary for Palestinians and Israelis to work together to achieve peaceful coexistence once a Palestinian state is established."[255] By February 2002, after a year and a half of unbearable suffering, the Palestinian majority was still striving only for its own liberation, and was not transforming its struggle into hatred and denial of the other side. This stands in sharp contrast to the official Israeli propaganda that "there is no partner for peace."

And on the other side of the barricades, opposition is mounting in Israel, and not just in terms of the cost of the occupation, but on moral grounds and the loss of human values. Most notable is Israeli draft resistance, there from the very first day of the uprising, but which has since grown and spread. At the end of January 2002, a group of reservists issued the following call, which has presently been signed by over four hundred reservists:

> We, reserve combat officers and soldiers of the Israel Defense Forces, who were raised upon the principles of Zionism, sacrifice and giving to the people of Israel and to the State of Israel, who have always served in the front lines, and who were the first to carry out any mission, light or heavy, in order to protect the State of Israel and strengthen it.... We hereby declare that we shall not continue to fight this War of the Settlements. We shall not continue to fight beyond the 1967 borders in order to dominate, expel, starve and humiliate an entire people. We hereby declare that we shall continue serving in the Israel Defense Forces in any mission that serves Israel's defense. The missions of occupation and oppression do not serve this purpose and we shall take no part in them.[256]

By February 2002, it seemed that for the first time, the idea of an immediate unilateral withdrawal was also beginning to gain support in the Israeli mainstream. Ami Ayalon, who comes from the heart of the security system (as former head of the Security Service), has had a significant effect. *Ha'aretz* reported that "After four months of intense discussion, the Council for Peace and Security, a group of 1,000 top-level reserve generals, colonels, and Shin Bet and Mossad officials, are [sic] to mount a public campaign for a unilateral Israeli withdrawal from all of Gaza and much of the West Bank.... About 80 percent of the full membership has signed on to the campaign.... Unlike some of the other unilateral withdrawal plans, like 'Life Fence,' for example, the council's plan involves evacuating some 40–50 settlements...."[257]

To judge by the polls, this solution has enormous popular support. Since mid-2002, the polls have shown a 60 percent or more majority in favor of dismantling settlements, even in the framework of a unilateral separation. The questions in the polls are not always unequivocal, but in a Dahaf poll on May 6, 2002, solicited by Peace Now, the questions were clear, and so were the answers: 59 percent of the Jewish Israelis support a unilateral withdrawal of the Israeli army from most of the occupied territories, and dismantling most of the settlements. They believe that this will renew the peace process, and this solution gives them hope.[258] These results were confirmed later by several other polls. The tens of thousands of Israelis who showed up at the demonstration of the peace coalition on May 11, 2002, responded to this call.

Nevertheless, this majority does not yet have a substantial political voice. Instead of calling for immediate withdrawal, the spokespeople for the peace camp are talking about separation and fences. Beilin's people are pushing to "resume negotiations" (while continuing to remain in the territories). In the big May 2002 demonstration, the speakers offered all kinds of ideas, except the one that most people wanted to hear—*get out now!* (Amos Oz spoke in that demonstration about continuing along the road of Camp David and Taba.) Although Peace Now conducted the survey mentioned above, and has a clear idea of what the majority wants, it abstains from calling for immediate withdrawal. In its vigils, people carry signs with the slogan: "GET OUT OF THE TERRITORIES!" but the word "NOW" is omitted.

The political leadership of the Israeli peace camp has years of experience diverting the majority of the occupation's opponents toward the route of preserving the status quo. These are the people who preached during the years of Oslo that the occupation was virtually over, and all we needed was just a few more years of negotiations. They are experts in convincing those who care to listen that the emperor is not naked, it is just some problem with our eyes. If the Israeli majority does not stay on guard, these experts may succeed again.

But for the first time since Oslo, there is also a growing Israeli peace movement that no longer obeys the political leaders of the peace camp. At its core, there are many local protest groups that became active from the onset of the uprising. This is the kernel of the Israeli left that did not get confused, and stood up immediately against the new phase of the occupation. Among them are Yesh-Gvul ("there is a limit")—the old draft resistance movement, which resumed activity in the first month of the Intifada and has already supported tens of its members in jail (via solidarity work, jail visits, letters, and financial support to the families); New Profile, a women's organization in support of draft resistance; the Coalition of Women for Just Peace, which comprises several women's organizations and whose members were demonstrating in Tel Aviv as early as October 1, 2000; Ta'ayush Arab-Jewish—a movement of Israeli Palestinians and Jews which focuses on solidarity work with the Palestinians in the occupied territories; Gush Shalom; Israeli members of the International Solidarity Movement; and many others.

A basic principle of these groups is that the movement for peace and against the occupation is a joint Israeli-Palestinian struggle. Right from the start, Israelis and Palestinians have co-organized peaceful demonstrations, extending hands to each other across the IDF's barricades and checkpoints. On the Palestinian side, more voices have gradually been heard calling for a return to a popular and civil uprising and away from armed struggle. Among these voices are Bir Zeit University and many others, calling to coordinate with Israeli anti-occupation activists, as in the previous uprising.

From the Palestinian diaspora, Edward Said phrased the

clear spirit of this message. In an article published in March 2001 he quotes Mandela's words: "The struggle of the Blacks in South Africa could attract the imagination and dreams of the entire world, because it offered the whole society—even the Whites who apparently benefited from the Apartheid—the only way that enables the preservation of basic human values." The Palestinian struggle, says Said, must be based on the understanding that the Jewish people are here to stay. The struggle must strive towards a settlement that will enable coexistence based on human dignity, a settlement that "will capture the imagination of the world."[259]

On the Israeli side, on March 20, 2001, 140 academics published an ad in three Palestinian newspapers that said: "We extend our arms to you in solidarity with your just cause...and wish to cooperate with you in opposing the IDF's brutal policy of siege, closure and curfews." In the spirit of Mandela and Said, they too believe that this cooperation "may serve as a precedent-setting example for future relations between the two communities in this country, our shared country."

On March 2001, in the village of Rantis near Tul Karem, I watched, bewildered, as approximately two hundred Israelis—youth along with old veterans—demolished with their bare hands the stone and earth barricade erected by the IDF—just one of the dozens of events of this kind that have taken place since the current round of Israeli oppression began. The people knew that as soon as they left, IDF bulldozers would return to reconstruct the barricade. Still, they looked happy. Because they knew that they too will be there again. They will be there for the only future worth living—a future based on basic human values.

THE OSLO APARTHEID

THE ERA OF YELLOW TERRITORIES
Ha'aretz Magazine, May 27, 1994.
by Tanya Reinhart, translated by Jeff Green.

In the past few weeks, many opponents of the occupation have been tempted to point out the resemblance between the end of apartheid in South Africa and the Gaza and Jericho agreements. However, if we look at the facts, setting aside feelings and hopes, the agreements with the PLO resemble the beginning of apartheid rather than its end. In 1959, the law promoting self-government of the Bantu peoples was passed in South Africa, institutionalizing the separation (apartheid) between whites and blacks. The reservations that were allocated to the blacks were declared self-governing entities and known generically as Bantustans.

The power in each of these entities was bestowed to local flunkies, and a few Bantustans even had elections, parliaments, or quasi-governmental institutions. However, foreign affairs, security, natural resources, and mines were carefully kept in the hands of the white regime. At first, the reservations had no independent sources of employment. The Bantustans were separated politically from South Africa, which controlled the entry of Bantustan residents into its territory. Officially, a permit was necessary to pass between any of these territories. Those who managed to acquire exit visas and work permits made their living working for white people under shameful conditions of exploitation. The workers returned to their homes at dusk or squatted in camps on the outskirts of the cities. Over the years, the cheap labor attracted foreign investors to establish industries in the Bantustans or near their borders. The Bantustans were allowed some symbols of sovereignty: a flag, postage stamps, passports, and a strong police force. The white regime strove to give the impression that the Bantustans were real countries, thus achieving a domestic political goal. All blacks were considered citizens of Bantustans, making them "foreigners" in South Africa and depriving them of their electoral and social rights.

The situation created by the Gaza and Jericho agreements, signed this May (1994) in Cairo, is almost identical. Of course, the Israeli peace camp is convinced that this is only a temporary agreement, the harbinger of a new era. However, the possibility that this arrangement may be frozen for years, or extended similarly to further areas of the West Bank cannot be ignored. According to Ze'ev Schiff, Arafat is convinced that "there will be no second stage after Gaza and Jericho. Therefore every kilometer and every small achievement is as important to him as if it were the last one."[260] Furthermore, those who still believe that Rabin's intentions are sincere, and that every detail of the exhausting, meticulous negotiations is intended for the short term only, must remember that in less than two years, after the next elections, the government may be replaced. In any case, this agreement is all we have, and the rest is pure hope. If so, what situation does this agreement create?

It leaves substantial parts of the Gaza Strip in Israel's hands. These areas are called "The Yellow Territories" on the maps accompanying the agreement. According to Mansour a-Shawa, candidate for head of the Gaza Council, the Palestinians will have autonomy over only 50 percent of the Gaza Strip lands.[261] The Yellow Territories include most of the land that is still available for construction and agriculture in the terribly overpopulated Gaza Strip. The Security Annex to the agreement forbids the Palestinians to build there and leaves planning and building in the Yellow Territories under Israel's control.[262] Gush Katif has, in fact, been excluded from the Gaza Strip, and the IDF has begun to build a NIS 35 million (New Israeli Shekels—the Israeli currency) electric fence in order to seal off the Gush Katif area.[263] Along with control over land, Israel has also retained control over water. The agreement preserves the exact situation that exists today. To solve the water shortage in Gaza, the Palestinians will be allowed to buy water from Israel. (Annex 2, paragraph 31.) Hence, the starting point for Gaza is worse than a Bantustan: neither water nor land.

During the years of occupation, Israel has neither developed nor allowed the development of an independent economic infrastructure in Gaza and the West Bank. The only real economic resource available today to the people of Gaza is employment in Israel. The economic agreement speaks eloquently of the "normal passage of workers" between both sides, "notwithstanding the right of each side to redefine from time to time the scale and conditions of the entry of workers into their area" (Chapter 7, paragraph 1)—impressive symmetry indeed. Considering the expected flow of Hebrew workers into the fields of Gaza, this actually means complete Israeli control over Gaza's workforce. As in a Bantustan, it is possible that entrepreneurs will be attracted by the cheap labor in the pressure cooker of Gaza, so that instead of importing workers into Israel, sweatshops will be built inside the Gaza Strip.

In any case, the interests of Israeli entrepreneurs have been protected. In the words of David Brodett, head of the Israeli economic delegation to the negotiations with the PLO, "On one issue our stand was firm: in the Cairo Agreements it was clearly stated that any discrimination against Israeli entrepreneurs, companies and Israel in general is strictly forbidden."[264] The economic agreement secures Israel's interests and the continuation of Gaza's economic dependence on Israel. One of the crises during the economic negotiations erupted after AbuAla proposed a free trade agreement between Gaza, Jericho, and Jordan, allowing the Palestinians to import cheaper products than those available through Israel. As with all other issues, Israel's objection was the final word. Even the meager Palestinian agricultural export to Israel was restricted with the convenience of Israeli farmers in mind. (Economical Agreements, Chapter 8, paragraph 10.) Thus, Gazastan can look forward to a future existence mainly as a source of cheap labor for Israeli and other entrepreneurs.

Nevertheless, Israel rejects any responsibility for the welfare of Gaza's citizens. Health care, social conditions, food shortages, and municipal services—all of the above are "internal affairs" of the Palestinians, now that they are sovereign. David Brodett explains frankly, "We are not being petty. When Israel withdraws from Gaza, the amounts the Local Administration budgeted for the month of May will remain in the local treasury.... This money should be sufficient for the day to day running of the Palestinian Authority for the first two or three weeks. After that, they are the boss."[265] At best, Israel is willing to reallocate the responsibility for the social welfare of residents living on the land it controls to charity organizations and international donors, who may or may not allocate billions to the benefit of the territories.

In the Bantustan spirit of "divide and rule," there is an evident trend toward complete separation among the different "autonomous" cantons. The agreement already institutionalizes such a separation between Gaza and the West Bank, allowing movement only between Jericho and the West Bank and only for the residents of those two areas. Supervision of this movement and the right to deny it remains in the hands of Israel. (Security Annex, "safe passage.") The spirit of these agreements is shown by the cancellation of thirteen hundred travel permits intended for students from the Gaza Strip. An appeal to the Supreme Court of Israel regarding this matter was rejected upon the request of the Attorney General. It is particularly interesting to note the rationales offered for this rejection. It was explained, for example, that these kinds of appeals are no longer relevant, since the Palestinian Authority is expected to deal with the internal issues in Gaza, education being one of these issues.[266] In other words, this is the logic of the "Peace Era": Now that the Palestinians have an independent government, the responsibility for their welfare is theirs. Somehow, waiting on line to receive flour from UNWRA, they should also solve their higher education problems. Meanwhile, if they are unable to study, that's obviously not our fault.

Ostensibly the legislative and judicial systems are areas in which the Palestinian Autonomy should have independent authority. However, even in these areas the agreement permits Israel's close supervision. All legislation must be confirmed by a joint "sub-committee for legal matters" and "within thirty days" of such legislation Israel can decide if the "legislation exceeds the judicial jurisdiction of the Palestinian Authority." (Agreement, part 7.3.) Furthermore, the agreement concludes that "Army rules and regulations that were valid before the Gaza and Jericho Agreements will remain so unless modified or canceled in accordance with this agreement." (Paragraph 7.9.) At this time, it seems that only seventy out of one thousand military edicts with which Israel controlled the strip will be canceled. Big Brother's eye will also watch the education system closely. "In accordance with the agreements of the civilian committees, Israel will be permitted to monitor Palestinian educational literature, to exclude any hostile material regarding Israel."[267]

Even if all of the above sounds like the usual occupation routine, the danger in the new situation lies in that from now on it will not be called occupation. Bantustan logic rules that now, after achieving a local authority, the Palestinians are also responsible for their own fate in the area of human rights. Even people with good intentions may be fooled by this. The Israeli Association for Civil Rights, for example, is currently debating whether it should continue to monitor human rights violations in the territories. "Where Israel is not sovereign, there is no place for association activity," says the head of the association, Amos Gil.[268]

Israel's control over the West Bank is entering a new and dangerous phase. We have not yet developed tools to deal with this situation. Indeed, how easy it is to submit to the feeling that the Palestinian problem is no longer Israel's, because the Palestinians have their own postage stamps and flag, police and travel documents. How easy it is to submit to the hope that the dynamics of things will work out on its own. Meanwhile, we shall sit at home and trust the government, because, after all, it is a peace government.

But the danger is that the Gaza and Jericho agreements may give Israeli occupation legal status, at least in these

Tanya Reinhart

areas. Since Arafat, who is thought to be the leader of the Palestinian national movement, signed this treaty of surrender, those who would like to may claim that the agreements were made with the approval of the Palestinian people. If so, the Security Council decisions 242 and 338 would no longer be valid, since the Palestinian people willingly approved of Israel's rule in exchange for autonomy. Although the agreement is called temporary, until a new one is achieved, only these arrangements will be valid in the eyes of international law.

The solution that may succeed remains the establishment of a true Palestinian state, and until we achieve that, we must be sure that a similar "temporary agreement" which institutionalizes Israeli control over the territories, disguised as self-government similar to a Bantustan, is not extended to the West Bank.

NOTES

1   Yeshayahu Leibowitz, "Territories," *Yediot Aharonot*, April 1968; reprinted in *Ha'aretz* March 16, 1969. (http://www.lei-bowitz.co.il)

2   For a concise history of U.S.-Israeli relations see Noam Chomsky's introduction to *The New Intifada—Resisting Israel's Apartheid* (Roane Carey, ed.) (London/New York: Verso, 2001). For a much more detailed history, see his *Fateful Triangle—The United States, Israel, and the Palestinians*, updated edition (Cambridge, Mass.: South End Press, 1999).

3   Robert Fisk, *Pity the Nation–Lebanon at War*, Oxford: Oxford University Press, 1990, p. 323

4   Hana Kim, *Ha'aretz*, November 10, 2000.

5   Edward Said, "Palestine Agenda," reprinted as Chapter 15 in his *The Politics of Dispossession* (New York: Vintage Books, 1994), 148. The article provides an extensive summary of the session's resolutions.

6   *Ha'aretz*, November 3, 1993.

7   For a fuller survey of the Oslo process, which I cannot cover here, see Noam Chomsky's "Washington's 'Peace Process'" in his *Fateful Triangle—The United States, Israel, and the Palestinians*, updated edition (Cambridge, Mass.: South End Press, 1999). Further information can be found in my columns,

which have appeared since 1994 in the Hebrew daily *Yediot Aharonot*, and are archived at: www.tau.ac.il/~reinhart/political/politicalE.html. (English translations for them start in 1996.)

8   Robert Malley, *The New York Times* and *Ha'aretz*, July 10, 2001.

9   Akiva Eldar, "On the Basis of the Nonexistent Camp David Understandings," *Ha'aretz*, November 16, 2000.

10 Hussein Agha and Robert Malley, "Camp David: The Tragedy of Errors," *The New York Review of Books*, August 9, 2001.

11 Beilin–Abu Mazen refers to the Israeli and Palestinian representatives Yossi Beilin and Abu Mazen (or Mahmoud Abbas). The complete text of the Beilin–Abu Mazen Plan is available online at: www.us-israel.org/jsource/Peace/beilinmazen.html.

12 Ze'ev Schiff, "Beilin's Final Agreement," *Ha'aretz*, February 23, 1996.

13 *Ha'aretz*, main headline, June 23, 2000. (Author's translation.)

14 Interview by Lili Galili, "I Want to Entangle the Likud with as Much Peace as Possible," *Ha'aretz*, March 3, 1996. (Author's translation.)

15 Uzi Benziman (analysis), *Ha'aretz*, June 23, 2000. (Author's translation.)

16 Ibid.

17 *Jerusalem Post*, August 18, 2000.

18 Amnon Kapeliouk, "Conducting Catastrophe," *Le Monde Diplomatique*, February 2002. The books surveyed are: Yossi Beilin, *A Manual for a Wounded Dove* (in Hebrew), (Tel Aviv: Yediot Aharonot Books, 2001); Gil'ad Sher, *Just Beyond Reach: The Israeli-Palestinian Peace Negotiations 1999-2001* (in Hebrew) (Tel Aviv: Yediot Aharonot Books, 2001); Shlomo Ben-Ami, *Quel avenir pour Israel?* (in French) (Paris: PUF, 2001).

19 Yossi Beilin, "Beilin Abu-Mazen with full responsibility," *Ha'aretz*, November 9, 2001.

20 The projected maps of Barak's plan and the Beilin Abu–Mazen's plan for the settlement blocs to be annexed are presented and analyzed in Danni Rubinstein, "Two maps which are hard to accept," *Ha'aretz*, January 28, 2000.

21 Nahum Barnea, *Yediot Aharonot*, June 30, 2000: "The Arabs living in the settlement blocks which will be annexed to Israel will have the same rights as the Israelis living in Palestine: They will vote to the Palestinian state and will live by its laws."

22 *Ha'aretz*, May 5, 1998. (Author's translation.)

23 For example, some headlines in the Israeli press: "Netanyahu Did Not Object to the Possibility That Abu Dis Will Be the Capital of Palestine" (Akiva Eldar, *Ha'aretz*, March 3, 2000); "Abu Dis Under Palestinian Control Also in Sharon's Map" (Akiva Eldar, *Ha'aretz*, May 1, 2000).

24 Eric Silver, *The Independent* (UK), May 15, 2000.

25 Nahum Barnea, "Abu Dis and Abu-pocket," *Yediot Aharonot* Saturday Supplement, May 12, 2000.

26 *Ha'aretz*, June 27, 2000.

27 Hussein Agha and Robert Malley, "Camp David: The Tragedy of Errors," *The New York Review of Books*, August 9, 2001.

28 Interview by Lili Galili, "I Want to Entangle the Likud with as Much Peace as Possible," *Ha'aretz*, March 3, 1996. (Author's translation.)

29 Howard Goller, Reuters, August 29, 2000.

30 *Jerusalem Post*, July 27, 2000.

31 *Ha'aretz*, June 7, 2000.

32   Shimon Shiffer, *Yediot Aharonot*, August 18, 2000.

33   The map was presented in the Eilat-Taba negotiations in May 2000, and was printed in *Yediot Aharonot* on May 19, 2000. Its English version here is taken from the July-August report of the Foundation for Middle East Peace, Washington, Vol. 10, No. 4 (www.fmep.org).

34   Shimon Shiffer, *Yediot Aharonot*, August 8, 2000.

35   *Ha'aretz*, January 15, 2001.

36   Gil'ad Sher was Barak's bureau chief, and was considered his confidant. He served as a top Israeli negotiator in the years 1999 through 2000. (See footnote 14.)

37   Shimon Shiffer, *Yediot Aharonot*, August 8, 2000.

38   Akiva Eldar, *Ha'aretz*, July 7, 2000.

39   *Jerusalem Post*, September 29, 2000.

40   For information on the Bantustans arrangement in South Africa, see the Appendix.

41   These are the numbers officially acknowledged in Israel, found, for example, in Uriya Shavit and Jalal Bana's "Everything you wanted to know about the 'right of return' but were too afraid to ask," *Ha'aretz* Friday Magazine, July 6, 2001. In other versions, the actual number of 1948 Palestinian refugees was higher.

42   The United Nations Relief and Works Agency for Palestine Refugees in the Near East (UNRWA)'s web site is at: www.un.org/unrwa/.

43   The complete text of UN General Assembly Resolution 194 is available at: www.un.org/Depts/dpa/qpal/docs/A_RES_194.htm.

44   For a history and survey of the right of return grassroots movements, see "Building The Movement of Return," an interview with Ingrid Jaradat by Toufic Haddad. *Between the Lines*, April

2001. www.between-lines.org.

45   Uri Avneri notes that "it is also worthwhile to remember that in 1949 the government of David Ben-Gurion and Moshe Sharett offered to take back 100 thousand refugees. Whatever the motives that inspired that offer, and even if this was merely a diplomatic maneuver, the offer is an important precedent. In relation to the Jewish population in Israel at that time, this number equals 800 thousand today. In relation to the number of refugees at that time, the number equals half a million now. The decisive question is: How many can be brought back? Minimalists may speak about 100 thousand, maximalists about half a million. I myself have proposed an annual quota of 50 thousand for 10 years. But this is a subject for negotiations, which must be conducted in a spirit of good-will with the intent of putting a successful end to this painful issue, always remembering that it concerns the fate of living human beings who deserve rehabilitation after tens of years of suffering." ("The Right of Return." See following footnote.)

46   Uri Avneri, "The Right of Return," Internet article, January 14, 2001. www.gush-shalom.org/old_archives.html.

47   Uriya Shavit and Jalal Bana, "Everything you wanted to know about the 'right of return' but were too afraid to ask," *Ha'aretz Friday Magazine*, July 6, 2001.

48   Ibid.

49   Ibid.

50   *Ha'aretz*, April 19, 1994.

51   *Yediot Aharonot*, December 10, 1999.

52   *Ha'aretz*, January 3, 2000.

53   *Yediot Aharonot*, January 3, 2000.

54 Quoted from *Ha'aretz*, January 13, 2000.

55 *Yediot Aharonot*, December 17, 1999.

56 Interview by Orly Azulai Katz, *Yediot Aharonot*, April 4, 2001.

57 Aluf Benn, *Ha'aretz*, July 27, 1999.

58 Amir Oren, *Ha'aretz*, January 14, 2000.

59 Robert Fisk, *The Independent* (UK), March 26, 2000.

60 Ibid.

61 Hussein Agha and Robert Malley, "Camp David: The Tragedy of Errors," *The New York Review of Books*, August 9, 2001.

62 Amir Oren, *Ha'aretz*, January 8, 1999.

63 Ibid.

64 Alex Fishman reported in *Yediot Aharonot* that the plans include an electronic fence, military posts on the border, new military camps, which require paving new roads, and a series of works protecting the villages and towns. If work is carried out day and night, the electronic fence will be completed in August/September 2000. All the rest has mostly not even started yet, and will take up to a year to complete. ("An electronic fence with a human back," *Yediot Aharonot*, Saturday Supplement, May 26, 2000.)

65 Tanya Reinhart, "Withdrawal?", *Yediot Aharonot*, May 29, 2000. www.tau.ac.il/~reinhart/political/politicalE.html.

66 Asaf Inbari, "The Stone Era," *Ha'aretz Friday Magazine*, September 29, 2000.

67 Ibid. (Author's translation.)

68 This was confirmed in reports of the Beilin–Abu Mazen plan, and Barak's revisions, in *Newsweek*, September 17, 2000, and *Ha'aretz*, September 18, 2000.

69 From an e-mailed report sent by LAW on September 28, 2000.

70 *Ha'aretz*, October 2, 2000.

71 Amir Oren, *Ha'aretz*, June 23, 2000.

72 See the complete text of LAW's Submission to the UN Human Rights High Commissioner, "LETHAL FORCE: Israel's Use of Military Force Against Palestinian Demonstrators," www.law-society.org/Reports/reports/2000/UNHCHR.htm.

73 *Ha'aretz*, January 6, 2002.

74 Amira Hass, *Ha'aretz*, January 30, 2001.

75 Report of Dr. Mustafa Barghouthi, the Union of Palestinian Medical Relief Committees, October 15, 2000.

76 *Ha'aretz*, November 1, 2000.

77 Associated Press, October 23, 2000.

78 *Yediot Aharonot*, October 27, 2000.

79 Ibid.

80 Amos Har'el, *Ha'aretz*, October 21, 2000.

81 Aluf Benn, *Ha'aretz*, July 22, 1999. (Author's translation)

82 This research was surveyed in Amnon Barzilai's "They didn't threaten London or Paris," *Ha'aretz*, June 23, 2000. (Author's translation.)

83 *Jerusalem Post*, October 24, 2000.

84 Ibid.

85 *Yediot Aharonot* Saturday Supplement, December 12, 2001.

86 Amir Oren, *Ha'aretz*, September 14, 2001.

87 Alex Fishman, *Yediot Aharonot*, October 19, 2001.

88 The first quote is from an interview with Amikam Rothman on radio B's morning program, October 24, 2000; the second, from

Ze'ev Schiff, *The 'Waiting Periods' of 1967 and 2001, Ha'aretz,* June 11, 2001.

89 "Those Who Have Not Finished the War of '48," *Ha'aretz,* May 3, 2001.

90 Interview by Ari Shavit, *Ha'aretz Friday Magazine,* April 13, 2001.

91 Amir Oren, "Truth or Consequences," *Ha'aretz,* November 17, 2000.

92 *IsraelWire,* September 12, 2000.

93 *Yediot Aharonot* Seven Days weekend magazine, November 11, 2000.

94 This section is taken from my article "Can't say we didn't know," *Yediot Aharonot,* November 14, 2000. www.tau.ac.il/~reinhart/political/politicalE.html.

95 LAW report, November 3, 2000.

96 *Ha'aretz,* November 5, 2000.

97 Associated Press, November 5, 2000.

98 *Ha'aretz,* November 5, 2000.

99 Addameer Report, November 4, 2000. Addameer—Prisoners' Support and Human Rights Association, Ramallah. www.addameer.org.

100 Dr. Jumana Odeh, Director, Palestinian Happy Child Center, October 24, 2000 report; LAW, November 2, 2000 report.

101 Dan Ephron, *Boston Globe,* November 4, 2000.

102 Arieh O'Sullivan, *Jerusalem Post,* October 27, 2000.

103 LAW report, October 19, 2000.

104 LAW report, November 2, 2000.

105 Arieh O'Sullivan, *Jerusalem Post*, October 27, 2000.

106 Ibid.

107 *Jerusalem Post*, October 30, 2000.

108 Charles M. Sennott, *Boston Globe*, May 3, 2001.

109 Ibid.

110 Masri, who comes from one of the wealthiest and most influential families in the West Bank city of Nablus, was the first prime
minister of Jordan to come from Palestinian territory, in the
early nineties. Interviewed by Christopher Dickey, *Newsweek*
Web exclusive, December 7, 2001. www.msnbc.com/news/NW-
front_Front.asp.

111 See Sara Roy, "Decline and Disfigurement: The Palestinian
Economy after Oslo," in *The New Intifada—Resisting
Israel's Apartheid*, Roane Carey (ed.), (London/New York:
Verso, 2001).

112 MIFTAH (the Palestinian Initiative for the Promotion of Global
Dialogue and Democracy), Intifada Update (No. 31), Palestinian
Human and Material Losses Inflicted by Israel during the
Intifada (Uprising) September 28, 2000, until December 24,
2001. www.miftah.org. There are often conflicting figures pro-
vided on human and material loss of the Palestinians. I use MIF-
TAH statistics throughout because its figures are usually the
most conservative.

113 MIFTAH: "Total income losses for Palestinian workers previously employed inside Israel: $3.6 million/day. Actual losses:
Shortfall in GNP between Sept.–Mar. $1.5 billion. Decrease in
per capita income: 47 percent."

114 "The Economic Price Paid by the Palestinians as a Result of the
Violence in the Territories," background paper prepared by
Operations Directorate, IDF Spokesperson Information and

Public Relations Branch, November 5 2000, distributed by Independent Media Review & Analysis). www.imra.org.il.

115 Ewen MacAskill, *The Guardian* (UK) June 28, 2001.

116 Eric Silver, *The Independent* (UK), November 7, 2000.

117 "The Economic Price Paid by the Palestinians as a Result of the Violence in the Territories," background paper prepared by Operations Directorate, IDF Spokesperson Information and Public Relations Branch, November 5, 2000, distributed by Independent Media Review & Analysis). www.imra.org.il.

118 "The Hidden Weapons Factories," *Ha'aretz*, December 12, 2001.

119 For history of Israel's death squad units see the official Israeli Special forces site: www.isayeret.com/217/article.htm. The document states proudly that "Israel has a long history in deploying undercover or 'Mistaravim' units. Mistaravim is the Hebrew term for becoming an Arab, which means not only to speak and to dress like one, but also to be well-familiar with the Arab customs and manners." The history dates back to pre-state days in the 1940's. The presently active unit, "Duvdevan" ('cherry'), was formed during the previous Palestinian Intifada, in the late eighties, and the document explains the need as follows: "In 1987, the Intifada—the Palestine uprising against the Israeli regime in the Occupied Territories—broke out. The Intifada was much different from the previous Palestinian resistance in 1970–1971. This time the IDF faced thousands of heavily armed terrorists [i.e., stone-throwing demonstrators] that enjoyed the full support of the local Palestinians. On the other hand, after years of occupation, Israel's media status wasn't good so deploying full-scale military force was impossible, especially when Israeli society was struggling within itself on the Intifada's legitimacy."

120 *Ha'aretz*, December 12, 2001.

121 Yoav Limor and Aryeh Bender, *Ma'ariv*, January 3, 2001.

122 Ron Ben Yishai, *Yediot Aharonot*, January 3, 2001.

123 See Peace Now's web site at: www.peacenow.org.il/English.asp.

124 Yehudit Har'el, Internet message, December 31, 2000.

125 Roni Shaked, *Yediot Aharonot*, December 12, 2001.

126 *Jerusalem Post*, October 25, 2000.

127 Daniel Sobleman, *Ha'aretz*, June 13, 2001.

128 Interviewed by Christopher Dickey, *Newsweek* Web exclusive, December 7, 2001. www.msnbc.com/news/NW-front_Front.asp.

129 Dr. Barghouthi is also the president of the Union of Palestinian Medical Relief Committees and has won the 2001 WHO World Health Award.

130 Dr. Mustafa Barghouthi, *The Palestinian Monitor*, December 19, 2001."

131 *Ha'aretz*, October 18, 2001.

132 *Ha'aretz*, December 5, 2001.

133 "Israel's Dead End," *Al Ahram Weekly*, December 20–26, 2001.

134 Independent (UK), December 15, 2001.

135 Associated Press, December 28, 2001.

136 *Ha'aretz*, December 14, 2001.

137 Details of this document were published in *Ma'ariv Weekend* supplement, July 6, 2001.

138 Shraga Eilam, "Peace With Violence or Transfer," "Between The Lines," December 2000. www.between-lines.org/archives/2000/dec/Shagra_Elam.htm. The major source is Anthony Cordesman, "Peace and War: Israel Versus the Palestinians: A Second Intifada?" Center for Strategic and

International Studies (CSIS), December 2000. The other source quoted in the paragraph above is David Eshel (a retired career officer in the IDF), "IDF Prepares for Palestinian Clashes," *Jane's Intelligence Review*, August 2000. These military plans were also discussed in the Israeli media over the years, e.g., by Amir Oren, *Ha'aretz*, November 23, 2001.

139 Quoted by Shraga Elam from Anthony Cordesman. (See previous footnote.)

140 Complete text of the document can be found at: www.gamla.org.il/english/feature/intro.htm.

141 Amir Oren, *Ha'aretz*, March 9, 2001.

142 *Yediot Aharonot*, March 9, 2001. For more on how the implementation of these plans began in March 2001, see my article "We Didn't See; We Didn't Know," *Yediot Aharonot*, March 14, 2001. www.tau.ac.il/~reinhart/political/politicalE.html.

In March 2001, Israel's plans were also mentioned in the U.S. press: "Plans to take back at least some of the territories from which Israeli troops began withdrawing in 1994 have been on the books for several years and are constantly reviewed. In the past few months, the army has undertaken an intensive effort to dust off and reevaluate these plans at the general command, battalion and brigade levels, sources said." (Lee Hockstader, *The Washington Post*, March 1, 2001.) At the time it was reported that the plans do not meet U.S. approval: "U.S. At the time, the reoccupation plan did not seem yet to meet U.S. approval: "In a preemptive move, the U.S. is warning Israel not to try to reoccupy territory controlled by the Palestinian Authority in attempts to curb attacks. Reoccupying some of the land turned over to the Palestinians...is an option said to be under consideration by the [Israeli] government. 'We've seen the report,' U.S. State Department spokesman Richard Boucher said yesterday.

'Obviously, we oppose actions that might exacerbate the situation.'" (Lamia Lahoud, *Jerusalem Post*, March 2, 2001.)

143 *Yediot Aharonot*, November 25, 2001.

144 Uzi Benziman, *Ha'aretz*, January 18, 2002.

145 *Ha'aretz*, February 9, 2002.

146 Ran Hacohen, "Killing and Taking Possession," antiwar.com, May 4, 2002. www.antiwar.com/hacohen/h050402.html.

147 Michael Jansen, *Jordanian Time*, October 5, 2001.

148 *The Guardian* (UK), October 12, 2001.

149 Aluf Benn, *Ha'aretz*, October 18, 2001.

150 Tanya Reinhart, "Evil Unleashed," *ZNet*, www.zmag.org, December 19, 2001. Also printed in *Tikkun*, Vol. 17, No. 2, March/April 2002.

151 Aluf Benn, *Ha'aretz*, March 19, 2002.

152 Lee Hockstader, *The Washington Post*, March 24, 2002.

153 "Bleak Horizons After Operation Defensive Wall," infopal, "The Independent Palestinian Information Network www.infopal.org, April 30, 2002.

154 Ibid.

155 Amir Oren, "At the gates of Yassergrad," *Ha'aretz*, January 25, 2002.

156 The refugee camp sits on a lot of approximately one square kilometer inside the city of Jenin. Its residents are mostly refugees who were driven out from Haifa and its vicinity in the 1948 war.

157 Tzadok Yehezkeli and Anat Tal Shir, "Down to Earth," *Yediot Aharonot* Seven Days weekend magazine, May 10, 2002.

158 "Word Games and Body Bags," by Irit Katriel, Indymedia Israel, April 21, 2002. www.indymedia.org.il/imc/israel/webcast.

159 Amos Har'el and Amira Hass, *Ha'aretz*, April 9, 2002. (Appeared only in the Hebrew edition.)

160 *Ha'aretz*, April 10, 2002.

161 Anat Zigelman and Aluf Ben, *Ha'aretz*, April 10, 2002. (Appeared only in the Hebrew edition.)

162 *Ha'aretz*, April 19, 2002, editorial column.

163 Ofer Shelah, *Yediot Aharonot* Saturday Supplement, April 19, 2002.

164 *Ha'aretz* staff and agencies, *Ha'aretz*, April 23, 2002.

165 Ibid.

166 Aluf Benn and Nathan Guttman, *Ha'aretz* April 24, 2002.

167 Shlomo Shamir, *Ha'aretz*, May 3, 2002.

168 Steve Weizman, Associated Press, May 6, 2002.

169 "Plaster" here refers to the adhesive bands used to secure gauze bandages to wounds. Suicide bombers frequently use the same material to adhere explosives to their bodies. However, Abdul Karim, the man in this account, was using the material to dress a wound.

170 Justin Huggler and Phil Reeves, *The Independent* (UK), April 21, 2002.

171 Rory MacMillan, *The Scotsman* (Scotland), April 8, 2002.

172 B'tselem, the Israeli Information Center for Human Rights in the Occupied Territories, April 12, 2002, daily report, www.b'tselem.org/english/press_releases/2002/updates/20020412.asp. A more updated report appeared in Hebrew as a supplement of *Ha'aretz* magazine, July 18, 2002.

173 Tsadok Yehezkeli and Anat Tal Shir, *Yediot Aharonot* Saturday Supplement, May 5, 2002.

174 Tsadok Yehezkeli, *Yediot Aharonot* Seven Days weekend magazine, May 31, 2002, translated from Hebrew by Gush Shalom.

175 Tsadok Yehezkeli, *Yediot Aharonot*, June 4, 2002, translated from Hebrew by Gush Shalom.

176 Jenin: IDF Military Operations, Human Rights Watch Report, Vol. 14, No. 3, May 2002, available at: http://hrw.org/reports/2002/israel3/.

177 Anat Zigelman, Amos Harel, and Amira Hass, *Ha'aretz*, April 12, 2002.

178 Amos Harel, Gideon Alon, and Jalal Bana, *Ha'aretz*, April 14, 2002.

179 Ibid.

180 Moshe Reinfeld and Anat Zigelman, *Ha'aretz*, Hebrew edition only, April 15, 2002.

181 Amos Harel, Gideon Alon, and Jalal Bana, *Ha'aretz*, April 14, 2002.

182 Amos Har'el, *Ha'aretz*, April 15, 2002.

183 Amos Har'el and Gideon Alon, *Ha'aretz*, April 15, 2002.

184 Aluf Benn, *Ha'aretz*, June 16, 2002.

185 *Ha'aretz* staff, *Ha'aretz*, June 25, 2002.

186 Yossi Verter, *Ha'aretz*, July 2, 2002.

187 Alex Fishman, *Yediot Aharonot* Saturday Supplement, March 9, 2001.

188 Aluf Benn, Amos Harel and Gideon Alon, *Ha'aretz*, June 23, 2002.

189 Nahum Barnea, *Yediot Aharonot*, June 21, 2002.

190 Amos Har'el, "The IDF Neutralizes the Palestinian Authority, and Humanitarian Organizations Try to Replace It," *Ha'aretz* (Hebrew edition only), June 23, 2002.

191 *Al Ahram Weekly*, March 28–April 3, 2002.

192 Justin Huggler, *The Independent* (UK), July 27, 2002.

193 Reported by Akiva Eldar, *Ha'aretz*, July 16, 2002.

194 Nathan Guttman and Yair Ettinger, *Ha'aretz*, August 6, 2002. The full report can be found at: www.usaid.gov/wbg/nutrition-al_report.pdf.

195 Amos Har'el, *Ha'aretz*, June 24, 2002.

196 Yair Ettinger, *Ha'aretz*, June 10, 2002.

197 Amos Har'el, *Ha'aretz*, Hebrew edition, June 23, 2002. (Quoted above.)

198 Nathan Guttman, *Ha'aretz*, June 29, 2002.

199 The campaign against UNRWA started earlier: "In letters written to Annan in May, Republican U.S. Senator Arlen Specter and Democratic U.S. Representative Tom Lantos accused the U.N. agency of allowing and promoting terrorist activity in the camps. Specter said UNRWA schools promoted anti Israeli and anti Semitic sentiments and Lantos said the agency allowed terrorists to organize in the camps," (Inter Press Service, June 24, 2002).

200 Interview with Michael Albert, *Znet* commentary, September 30, 2001, partially reprinted in Noam Chomsky, *9-11* (New York: Seven Stories Press, 2001), 94.

201 "The Algebra of Infinite Justice," *The Guardian*, UK, Sept. 29, 2001.

202 *Ha'aretz*, December 12, 1997. (Author's translation)

203 This is taken from an article of mine in *Yediot Aharonot:* "The A-Sherif Affair," April 14, 1998. Complete text available at: www.tau.ac.il/~reinhart/political/A_Sharif.html.

204 Roni Shaked, "The Escape Route of the Murderers," *Yediot Aharonot* Saturday Supplement, April 3, 1998.

205 *Yediot Aharonot*, April 5, 1998.

206 *Ha'aretz*, April 6, 1998. (Author's translation.)

207 *Ha'aretz*, April 7, 1998.

208 *Ha'aretz*. April 7, 1998. (Author's translation.)

209 Danni Rubinstein, "A Mystery That Did Not Exist," *Ha'aretz*, April 3, 1998.

210 According to Basam Id, *Ha'aretz*, April 12, 1998.

211 *Ha'aretz*, April 14, 1998.

212 *Kol ha-Ir* (Jerusalem Hebrew weekend magazine), "This Is How the CIA Operates in Israel and in the Territories," November 24, 2000.

213 David Hirst, "Arafat's Last Stand?" *The Guardian* (UK), December 14, 2001. For more on Arafat's corrupt rule see my *Yediot Aharonot* articles "Mandela He Ain't," May 25, 1994; "Arafat's Return to Gaza," July 7, 1994; "The Road of Collaboration," April 7, 1997. www.tau.ac.il/~reinhart/political/politicalE.html.

214 Interview with Ari Shavit, *Ha'aretz* Weekend Magazine, April 13, 2001.

215 The interview was published more than twenty years later in *Yediot Aharonot*, April 27, 1997. In the 1973 Yom Kippur War, for the first time Israeli society paid a heavy price for its occupa-

tion. The interview with Dayan was held three years after the defeat, and in that atmosphere, he explained that the decision to attack Syria was a mistake that would disable peace with Syria in the future.

216 Ibid.

217 For details and references, see Noam Chomsky, *The Fateful Triangle* (Cambridge, Mass.: South End Press, 1983, 1999), 97, 132-133.

218 Amnon Kapeliouk, Yitzhak Rabin interview, "1983: New Opportunities for Peace," *Trialogue*, Winter 1983. Quoted in Noam Chomsky, *The Fateful Triangle* (Cambridge, Mass.: South End Press, 1983, 1999).

219 *Ha'aretz*, January 8, 1999. (See Chapter IV.)

220 Complete text of the article (in Hebrew) can be found at: www.tau.ac.il/~reinhart/political/01GovmntObstacleToPeace.d oc. Extended version appeared (in Hebrew) in *Noga 27*, April 1994, titled "Peace, Peace, and No Peace."

221 Interview in *Yediot Aharanot* Saturday Supplement, December 7, 2001.

222 Cited in Amira Lam and Avner Hofstein, "Profile: The Deputy Chief of Staff, Maj. Gen. Moshe (Bugi) Ya'alon," *Yediot Aharonot* Seven Days weekend magazine, June 1, 2001. The debate between the Military Intelligence (Am'an) and the Security Service (Shin Bet) continued in the first year of the Palestinian uprising (when Am'an was headed by Amos Malka, and Shin Bet by Avi Dichter). Formally they differed on the question of whether Arafat has full control and whether or not he could stop terrorism if he wanted (Am'an's position), or he if has only partial control and limited ability (Shin Bet's position). (See, e.g., Amir Oren, *Ha'aretz*, May 20, 2001; Amos

Har'el, *Ha'aretz*, June 6, 2001.) But the real content underlying this pseudo-debate was whether Arafat and the PA should be toppled (Am'an), or some sort of the Oslo arrangements should be renewed (Shin Bet). However, in later months, Shin Bet adopted Am'an's position.

223 Amir Oren, *Ha'aretz*, November 17, 2000.

224 *Yediot Aharonot*, November 7, 2000.

225 Richard Sale, Washington, UPI, March 1, 2001.

226 To cite just a few examples, leaders of the Shin Bet (Security Service) and the Military Intelligence, met regularly with the U.S. ambassador and fed him information about Arafat's responsibility for acts of terrorism (Amir Oren, "Natanya Reflex," *Ha'aretz*, May 20, 2001). Alex Fishman reports that since October 2001, the security echelon "has been exposing classified intelligence information to international bodies, like the European Union, the UN, Norway, Italy, and, of course the US...Security sources declare: 'We will prove to the world that Arafat is a liar.' And indeed, this works..." (*Yediot Aharonot* Saturday Supplement, November 2, 2001). The army not only determines the military moves, but advises the government regarding the political conditions for their realization, including when it is good to show temporary "restraint": "The Israel Defense Forces General Staff will tell Prime Minister Ariel Sharon and Defense Minister Binyamin Ben-Eliezer next week that the government should show restraint in the next few weeks...until two upcoming events have passed: the Arab summit and Sharon's visit to Washington in a month's time." (Amir Oren, *Ha'aretz*, March 9, 2001.)

227 *Yediot Aharonot*, November 7, 2000.

228 Alex Fishman, *Yediot Aharonot*, October 19, 2001.

229 Peres has disclosed this several times, e.g.: "Peres accused the army of a mud-slinging campaign to undermine him and said that Maj-Gen Ya'alon would like to physically eliminate Mr Arafat," *Daily Telegraph* (UK), October 2, 2001.

230 UPI, March 1, 2001.

231 *Ha'aretz*, October 19, 2001.

232 *Ha'aretz*, March 23, 2001.

233 Aluf Benn, *Ha'aretz*, December 18, 2001.

234 Ed Vulliamy, *The Observer* (UK), September 30, 2001.

235 Amos Harel, *Ha'aretz*, December 24, 2001.

236 Amir Oren, *Ha'aretz*, July 9, 2002.

237 *Le Monde*, December 17, 2001.

238 A reply to Benny Morris, *The Guardian* (UK), February 22, 2002.

239 Yoni Ben Menachem, Israel Radio, January 20, 2001.

240 Aluf Benn , *Ha'aretz*, January 28, 2001.

241 Ben Caspit, *Ma'ariv*, January 23, 2001.

242 *Jerusalem Post*, online news, January 24, 2001.

243 Nahum Barnea, *Yediot Aharonot*, December 29, 2000.

244 Ben Caspit, *Ma'ariv*, January 4, 2001.

245 *Yediot Aharonot*, December 29, 2000.

246 Nahum Barnea, *Yediot Aharonot*, December 29, 2000.

247 Ibid.

248 This is openly explained in the Israeli media. For example, *Ha'aretz* conservative commentator Nehemia Strasler, alarmed by the economic effects of the present "state of war," explains the benefits of the peace negotiations policy which started with Oslo: "The turning point for the Israeli economy was on

September 13, 1993, when Yitzhak Rabin signed the Oslo agreement. Within a short time, the world changed its attitude toward Israel. From a state that appeared on television screens as a country at war, Israel was transformed into a site of pilgrimage. The Arab boycott was canceled, 30 states renewed their diplomatic relations with Israel, foreign investments reached the level of several billion dollars a year, exports went to countries where Israel previously did not have a foothold, and the Israeli economy began to grow at the dizzying rate of 7.0 % in 1994 and 6.8 % in 1995, with unemployment declining to a welcome low of 6.6 % of the work force." ("The Arithmetic of War," *Ha'aretz*, February 22, 2002.)

249 *Ha'aretz*, January 29, 2001.

250 Dahaf Institute poll supervised by Dr. Mina Zemach, *Yediot Aharonot* Saturday Supplement, December 12, 1997.

251 *Yediot Aharonot*, February 22, 2002.

252 For more on the interesting blank ballot struggle in Israel, see my article "The blank ballot strategy," *Zed* magazine, September 1996, and later articles in *Yediot Aharonot*. Translations can be found at: www.tau.ac.il/~reinhart/political/politicalE.html.

253 The opening paragraphs here are from my article "Out now!" *Yediot Aharonot*, July 8, 2001.

254 Interviewed by Alain Cypel, *Le Monde*, December 22, 2001.

255 The survey of 1,198 respondents was held February 7 through 9 in seventy-five Palestinian communities in the West Bank, the Gaza Strip, and East Jerusalem. Its report (Palestinian Public Opinion Poll # 6) can be found at: http://home.birzeit.edu/dsp/polls/p6/. A summary was also given by Amira Hass, *Ha'aretz*, February 19, 2002.

256 This text and further information can be found at the group's site: www.seruv.org.il/defaultEng.asp.

257 Lili Galili, *Ha'aretz*, February 18, 2002.

258 *Ha'aretz* online, May 10, 2002 ('Poll: 59% say W. Bank, Gaza exit would renew peace process,' by The Associated Press). Full results can be found at: www.peacenow.org/Campaign2002/PollMay2002.rtf.

259 Edward Said, "The Only Alternative," March 8, 2001, *ZNet* Commentary. www.zmag.org/ZNET.

260 *Ha'aretz*, May 8, 1994.

261 *Ha'aretz*, May 5, 1994.

262 Summary of the Annex, *Ha'aretz* May 5, 1995.

263 *Ha'aretz*, April 24, 1994.

264 *Yediot Aharonot*, May 6, 1994.

265 Ibid.

266 *Ha'aretz*, May 6, 1994.

267 Attorney Rajah Surani to Amira Hass, *Ha'aretz*, May 9, 1994.

268 *Ha'aretz*, May 11, 1994.

INDEX

266

Tanya Reinhart

Tanya Reinhart

Tanya Reinhart

Popular Front for the Liberation of
Palestine (PFLP), 122
poverty, Palestinian, 119–121
Powell, Colin, 143, 144, 157–158
press. *See* media
propaganda, Israeli. *See also* "White
Book"
about Arafat, 135, 181–182
analogy to 1948, 111
Israeli army, 199
Jenin refugee camp, 153–156, 158
military power, 196–197
peace, 230
public opinion, Israeli
assassination, 123
Golan Heights, 87, 224
Israeli withdrawal, 231–232
Lebanon, 82
October 2000 events, 110–111
Oslo Accords, 15–16
peace, 223–224
public opinion, Palestinian
Israel, 14–15
peace, 229–230

Al-Quds, 26–27, 34–35, 36, 38, 215.
See also Abu-Dis
Qurei, Othman Muhamad, 36–37

Rabbani, Mouin, 148–149, 150–151
Rabin, Yitzhak
Alon plan, 191, 192–193
assassination, 26
and Dugit settlers, 46
endless negotiations concept, 72
Gaza and Jericho agreements, 238
on Gaza Strip, 16
and Hebron settlers, 47
Israeli-Syrian negotiations, 62–63
Oslo negotiations, 18

"redemption of land" myth, 188
and Syria, 190
racism, and October 2000 events,
110–111. *See also* ethnic
cleansing
Rajub, Gibril, 183, 184, 186
Rantis, 234–235
al-Rantisi, Abdel Azis, 186
Raz, Sgt., 113–114
Red Crescent, 153, 168
"redemption of land" myth,
188–191, 194, 227
Reeves, Charles, 131
rehabilitation, physical, 115–116
Reuters, 186
right of return, 51–60, 215–216,
218–219, 227–228
Ron, Alik, 107–108
Ross, Dennis, 72
Roy, Arundhati, 180
Rumsfeld, Donald, 143, 205

Sadat, Anwar, 65, 189
Said, Edward, 15, 130, 234
Sale, Richard, 202
Salfit, 131
Sarena, Yigal, 101–102
Sarid, Yossid, 85, 210
Schiff, Ze'ev, 106, 238
Schiffer, Shimon, 147
separation model, 173–176
settlement blocs, 33, 56, 214, 227
settlements, leasing, 217–218
Sha'at, Nabil, 17
Shaba Farms, 86–87
Shafi, Haidar Abd-el, 17
Shahak, Amnon, 198
Shai, Nahman, 135
Shaked, Roni, 182
Shalabi, Fathi, 158–159

Tanya Reinhart

ABOUT THE AUTHOR

Tanya Reinhart is a professor of linguistics and cultural studies at Tel Aviv University and the University of Utrecht. Academically, she is best known for her contribution to theoretical linguistics. Following the Oslo agreements in 1994—which she viewed as a painful deception of the Palestinian people and the implementation of a sophisticated Israeli apartheid regime—she turned to political writing. She contributes a regular critical column to *Yediot Aharonot*, Israel's biggest daily, and publishes widely online and in the international media. For more information about Tanya Reinhart, visit her web site: www.tau.ac.il/~reinhart.